LITERATURE

This edition published by Lector House in 2024

ISBN: 978-93-6138-772-2

Lector House LLP
Registered Office: H. No. 96, Block C, Tomar Colony,
Burari, Delhi – 110084, India
info@lectorhouse.com
www.lectorhouse.com

LITERATURE

DEPARTMENT OF EDUCATION, ONTARIO

2024

LECTOR HOUSE

LECTOR HOUSE LLP

ONTARIO TEACHERS' MANUALS

LITERATURE

AUTHORIZED BY

THE MINISTER OF EDUCATION

CONTENTS

CHAPTER III

CHAPTER IV
FORM I: SENIOR GRADE

CHAPTER V
FORM II

CHAPTER VI
FORM III

CHAPTER VII
FORM IV

CHAPTER VIII

CHAPTER IX

PUBLIC AND SEPARATE SCHOOL—COURSE OF STUDY—DETAILS

FORM I

A. Selections from The Ontario Readers

B. Supplementary Reading and Memorization: Selection may be made from the following:

I. *To be Read to Pupils:*

1. Nursery Rhymes: Sing a Song of Sixpence; I Saw a Ship a-Sailing; Who Killed Cock Robin; Simple Simon; Mary's Lamb, etc.

   Consult *Verse and Prose for Beginners in Reading;* Riverside Literature Series, No. 59, 15 cents.

2. Fairy Stories: Briar Rose, Snow-white and Rose-red—Grimm; The Ugly Duckling—Andersen; Cinderella, The Sleeping Beauty in the Wood—Perrault; Beauty and the Beast—Madame de Villeneuve; The Wonderful Lamp—Arabian Nights' Entertainments.

   Consult *Fairy Tales Every Child Should Know,* by H. W. Mabie. Grosset & Dunlap, 50c.

3. Folk Stories: Whittington and His Cat; The Three Bears.

4. Fables: Selections from Æsop and La Fontaine.

   Consult *Fables and Folk Stories,* by Scudder, Parts I and II; Riverside Literature Series, Nos. 47, 48, 15 cents each.

II. *To be Read by Pupils:*

Fables and Folk Stories—Scudder; A Child's Garden of Verses (First Part)—Stevenson; Readers of a similar grade.

III. *To be Memorized by Pupils:*

1. Memory Gems: Specimens of these may be found in the Public School Manuals on Primary Reading and Literature.

2. From the Readers: Morning Hymn; Evening Prayer; The Swing; What I Should Do; Alice.

FORM II

A. Selections from Second Reader

B. Supplementary Reading and Memorization: Selection may be made from the following:

I. *To be Read to Pupils:*

1. Narrative Poems: John Gilpin—Cowper; Lucy Gray—Wordsworth; Wreck of the Hesperus—Longfellow; Pied Piper of Hamelin—Browning; May Queen—Tennyson; etc.

   Consult *The Children's Garland,* Patmore. The Macmillan Co., 35 cents.

2. Nature Stories: Wild Animals I Have Known, Lives of the Hunted—Thompson-Seton; The Watchers of the Trails—Roberts.

3. Fairy Stories: Fairy Tales Every Child Should Know—H. W. Mabie.

4. Other Stories: Selections from the Wonder Book—Hawthorne; Jungle Book—Kipling; Gulliver's Travels—Swift; Alice in Wonderland—Carroll; Robinson Crusoe—Defoe; The Hall of Heroes—Royal Treasury of Story and Song, Part III, Nelson & Sons.

II. *To be Read by Pupils:*

A Child's Garden of Verses—Stevenson; The Seven Little Sisters—Jane Andrews; Fifty Famous Stories Retold—Baldwin.

III. *To be memorized by Pupils:* (A minimum of six lines a week)

From the Reader:

A Wake-up Song; Love; The Land of Nod; One, Two, Three; March; Abide with Me; The New Moon; The Song for Little May; The Lord is my Shepherd; Lullaby—Tennyson; Indian Summer; proverbs, maxims, and short extracts found at the bottom of the page in the Readers.

FORM III

A. Selections from Third Reader

B. Supplementary Reading and Memorization: Selection may be made from the following:

The King of the Golden River—Ruskin; Tanglewood Tales—Hawthorne; The Heroes—Kingsley; Adventures of Ulysses—Lamb; Squirrels and Other Fur-bearers—Burroughs; Ten

Little Boys who Lived on the Road from Long Ago till Now—Jane Andrews; Hiawatha—Longfellow; Rip Van Winkle—Irving; Water Babies—Kingsley.

To be Memorized by Pupils: (A minimum of ten lines a week)

FROM THE READER:

To-day—Carlyle; The Quest—Bumstead; Hearts of Oak—Garrick; A Farewell—Kingsley; An Apple Orchard in the Spring—Martin; The Charge of the Light Brigade—Tennyson; Lead, Kindly Light—Newman; The Bugle Song—Tennyson; Crossing the Bar—Tennyson; The Fighting Téméraire—Newbolt; Afterglow—Wilfred Campbell; proverbs, maxims, and short extracts.

FORM IV

A. SELECTIONS FROM FOURTH READER

B. SUPPLEMENTARY READING AND MEMORIZATION: Selections may be made from the list prepared annually by the Department of Education.

LITERATURE

CHAPTER I

INTRODUCTION

It is the purpose of this Manual to present the general principles on which the teaching of literature is based. It will distinguish between the intensive and the extensive study of literature; it will consider what material is suitable for children at different ages; it will discuss the reasons for various steps in lesson procedure; and it will illustrate methods by giving, for use in different Forms, lesson plans in literature that is diverse in its qualities. This Manual is not intended to provide a short and easy way of teaching literature nor to save the teacher from expending thought and labour on his work. The authors do not propose to cover all possible cases and leave nothing for the teacher's ingenuity and originality.

WHAT IS LITERATURE?

Good literature portrays and interprets human life, its activities, its ideas and emotions, and those things about which human interest and emotion cluster. It gives breadth of view, supplies high ideals of conduct, cultivates the imagination, trains the taste, and develops an appreciation of beauty of form, fitness of phrase, and music of language. The term *Literature* as used in this Manual is applied especially to those selections in the *Ontario Readers* which possess in some degree these characteristics. Such selections are unlike the lessons in the text-books in grammar, geography, arithmetic, etc. In these the aim is to determine the facts and the conclusions to which they lead. Even in the Readers, there are some lessons of which this is partly true. For instance, the lesson on *Clouds, Rains, and Rivers*, by Tyndall, is such as might be found in a text-book in geography or science. Here the information alone is viewed as valuable, and the pupil will probably supplement what he has learned from the book by the study of material objects and natural phenomena. When this lesson is to be studied, the pupil should be taught not only to understand thoroughly what the author is expressing by his language, but also to appreciate the clearness and force with which he has given his message to the world. The pupil should be called upon to examine the author's illustrations, his choice of words, and his paragraph and sentence structure.

Each literature lesson in the Reader has some particular force, or charm of thought and expression. There is found in these lessons, not only beauty of thought and feeling, but artistic form as well. In the highest forms of literature, the emotional element predominates, and it should be one to which all mankind, to a greater or less degree, are subject. It is the predominance of these emotional and artistic elements which makes literature a difficult subject to teach. The element of feeling is elusive and can best be taught by the influence of contagion. There is usually less difficulty about the intellectual element, that is, about the meaning of words and phrases, the general thought of the lesson, and the relation of the thoughts to one another and to the whole.

THE QUALITIES THAT APPEAL TO CHILDREN AT DIFFERENT AGES

This is a psychological problem which can be solved only by a study of the interests and capacities of the children. These interests vary so greatly and make their appearance at such diverse periods in different individuals and in the two sexes, that it is a difficult matter to say with any definiteness just what qualities of literature appeal to children at any particular age. Moreover, the children's environment and previous experiences have a great deal to do in determining these interests and capacities. There are, however, certain characteristics of different periods of childhood which are fairly universal, and which may, therefore, be taken as guiding, determining factors in the selection of suitable literature.

In Junior Forms

1. One of the most striking characteristics of young children is the activity of their imagination. They endow their toys with life and personality; they construct the most fantastic and impossible tales; they accept without question the existence of supernatural beings. The problem for the teacher is to direct this activity of imagination into proper fields, and to present material which will give the child a large store of beautiful images—images that are not only delightful to dwell upon, but are also elevating and refining in their influence upon character. The fairy tale, the folk tale, and the fable, owe their popularity with young children to the predominance of the imaginative element. The traditionary fairy tales and folk stories are usually more suitable than those that appear in teachers' magazines and modern holiday books for children. The hardest thing for the educated mind to do is to write down to the level of children without coddling or becoming cynical. The old tales are sincere, simple, and full of faith. They are not written for children, but are the romance of the people with whom they came into existence, and they have stood the test of ages.

The myth is usually not suitable for young children, as it is a religious story having a symbolic meaning which is beyond their interpretation. If it is used at all, only the story in it should be given.

2. Stories of adventure, courage, and the defence of the helpless appeal very strongly to young children. Even the cruelties and crudities of *Bluebeard, Ali Baba and the Forty Thieves,* and *Aladdin and his Wonderful Lamp* do not alarm or repel children very much, owing to their lack of experience in these matters. Stories based on the love of the sexes are unsuitable for children of this age, although it

constitutes the chief element in stories for older people.

3. The child is also interested in stories of simple games, of animals and birds, and of the material world on which so much of his happiness depends. These stories are corrective of the desire which characterizes some children for too many fairy stories. The fairy story and the nature story should be alternated, so that the child's interests may be imaginative without becoming visionary, and practical without becoming prosaic.

4. Most children have a keen sense of the musical qualities of verse. The child of two years of age will give his attention to the rhythm of the nursery rhyme when the prose story will not interest him. The consideration and analysis of these musical qualities should be deferred for years; but it is probable that the foundation for a future appreciation of poetry is often laid by an acquaintance with the rhymes of childhood.

5. The element of repetition appeals strongly to children. In this lies the attractiveness of the "cumulative story", in which the same incident, or feature, or form of expression is repeated again and again with some slight modification; for example, the story of *Henny Penny, The Gingerbread Boy*, and *The Little Red Hen*. The choruses and the refrains of songs are pleasant for this reason.

Silverlocks and the Three Bears is an example of a story that has many attractive features. Silverlocks is an interesting girl, because she is mischievous and adventurous. The pupils know a good deal about bears and wild animals from picture books, stories, and perhaps the travelling menageries. The bears have all proper names—Rough Bruin, Mammy Muff, and Tiny; this gives an air of reality to the story. The bears speak in short, characteristic sentences.

Silverlocks runs away from home, goes into the woods, and finds a lonely house which is the home of the bears. They are not at home, so she enters. These actions suggest mystery and adventure.

The construction of the story shows two chief divisions, with three subdivisions. The second division begins with the return of the bears. They find the soup has been tasted, the chairs disturbed, and the beds rumpled; their conversation is interesting, and their tones characteristic. Tiny, the little bear, suffers most; he enlists the sympathy of the children, as he has lost his dinner and his chair is broken. He discovers Silverlocks, but she escapes and "never runs away from home any more".

In Senior Forms (Books III and IV)

1. In these Forms, the pupil's imagination is still strong, though less fantastic and under better control, and hence stories involving a large element of imagination retain their charm at this stage. The myth, and longer and more involved fairy tales, such as Ruskin's *King of the Golden River*, Hawthorne's *Wonder Book*, and Kingsley's *Greek Heroes*, are read with avidity.

2. Stories involving *a number of incidents* are wonderfully attractive. This is due to the pupil's instinctive interest in action and personality. Children are more

deeply interested in persons who *do* things than in those who *become* something else than they were. A description of some evolution of character very soon palls, but a stirring tale of heroic deeds exerts a powerful fascination. This explains the attractiveness of the hero tale, the story of adventure, and the stirring historical narrative. The action should have the merit of artistic moderation. Stories in which there is a carnival of action, for example, the "dime thriller", under whose spell so many boys fall, must be avoided. Literature that leaves the mind so feverish that the pupil loses interest in other subjects is worse than no literature. The easiest way to prevent a taste for this injurious kind, is to give the pupil an acquaintance with works descriptive of noble deeds and virile character. An interest in epic poetry or the historical novel may be developed from the child's instinctive interest in action. Tennyson's *Passing of Arthur*, Arnold's *Sohrab and Rustum*, Longfellow's *Evangeline* and *King Robert of Sicily*, and Scott's *Ivanhoe* will be read with keen enjoyment. The force and beauty of the language, the faithfulness of the descriptions to life, the historical setting, the lofty imagery, and the logical development will arouse a healthy mental appetite that will find no pleasure in the worthless story of sensation and vulgar incident, or even in some badly constructed compositions of historical adventure.

3. The pupils of the Senior Forms show even more striking interest in animals, pets, and wild creatures than do the pupils of the Junior Forms. To this natural interest is due the engrossing character of nature study. To it is also due the satisfaction arising from the reading of some of the many nature stories that have appeared in recent years.

Thompson-Seton's *Wild Animals I have Known* and *Lives of the Hunted*, and Roberts' *The Watchers of the Trails* are excellent examples of this class.

Complete Wholes versus Extracts

Scattered throughout the *Ontario Readers* are to be found extracts from larger works. These extracts are placed there primarily because they have some special literary value. They have fairly complete unity in themselves and can be treated in detail in a way that would be impossible with a whole story. The extract has an advantage over the whole, in that it repays intensive study, while, in many cases, such study of the whole work would not be worth while. It is considered better to give the pupil many of these passages where the author has shown his greatest art, rather than to allow one long work to absorb the very limited time which the pupil can devote to this subject. The study of the extract will have accomplished its mission if it induces the pupil to read the larger work for himself in later years. If the treatment by the teacher is made as interesting as it should be, it is hoped that the pupil will obtain such delight from, and be inspired to such enthusiasm by, these glimpses of literary treasures, that he will not be satisfied until he has enjoyed in their entirety such works as *The Lady of the Lake, Pickwick Papers, Lorna Doone, The Mill on the Floss, Julius Cæsar,* and *It is Never Too Late to Mend*. An extract may serve as an introduction to the choicest work of an author, may arouse an interest in his writings, and give the pupils a taste of his quality, but, unless it whets their appetites for the work as a whole, its chief purpose will not have been accomplished.

These extracts cannot give a panoramic view of a great historical epoch. They do not require that sustained attention that relates to-day's readings with that of yesterday, and that takes a wider survey of many parts in their relation to a central theme. The larger work gives a culture and a liberal education, when it is treated in the proper manner, that is very different from the fragmentary knowledge of an author that would be gained by even the intensive study of many short extracts. The treatment of the extract, as we have said, must be minute; while the whole work should be subsequently read in a method that will be outlined later on under the head of Supplementary Reading.

Correlation of Literature with Nature Study, Geography, History, and Art

Many of the lessons in the *Ontario Readers* should be preceded by preparatory work in geography, history, or nature study. Poems such as *Jacques Cartier, The Charge of the Light Brigade, The Burial of Sir John Moore,* and *The Armada* cannot be fully appreciated unless the historical setting is known. There are famous pictures that will increase the pupil's interest in these poems. In the lessons on art, there are studies of pictures that suggest feelings and thoughts characterized by universality, permanency, and nobility—pictures that stir men to nobler thought and higher aspiration. Often, such pictures are the painter's method of expressing in colours, thoughts that the poet has expressed in words. Lessons such as *Dandelions, Bob White,* and *The Sandpiper* require a preliminary acquaintance with certain facts of nature, and therefore should be taken, if possible, when these can be obtained through personal observation by the pupils. *Wolfe and Montcalm* and Drake's *Voyage Around the World* demand, in addition to historical facts, certain geographical data. These facts and data should be communicated at some time before the lessons in literature are taken, in order that the latter may not descend into lessons in history, geography, or natural science. The extracts mentioned above are not placed in the Readers to teach certain historical, geographical, or scientific facts. They are placed there, as has been said, primarily because they have some value as literature. Hence the literature lesson should require few digressions, the necessary preparatory work having been done in previous periods.

But while history, geography, nature study, and art frequently assist in the interpretation of a poem or prose selection, these subjects, on the other hand, may be reinforced and strengthened by selections drawn from the fields of literature. The facts of the history lesson will be given an additional attractiveness if the pupil is directed to some well-written biography or drama embodying the same facts, or if the teacher reads or recites to the class some spirited ballad, such as *Bonnie Dundee,* bearing upon the lesson. The interest in the observations made in nature study will be intensified by reading some nature story written in good literary form.

While these studies may go hand in hand with literature, it is not necessary that they should be always taken on the same day or even in the same week. The literature lesson may be an effective agent in the recall of ideas that have had time to be assimilated from previous nature study, history, or geography lessons. In our enthusiasm for literature we must not make these subjects the mere soil and fertilizers out of which the flowers of poetry will spring. Each of these subjects has its proper sphere, but that teacher misses many golden opportunities who does not frequently take a comprehensive survey of his material in all these studies in order to find the element that will give a unity to all our knowledge and experience. The lessons in the Reader may be taken according to the conditions existing in the class or the inclination of the teacher. By no means is it necessary to follow the order in the book.

Aims in Teaching Literature

The teacher should always have a clear and definite aim in view in teaching a selection in literature, but different teachers may have different aims in teaching the same selection. There should, of course, always be the general aim to create a taste for good literature by leading the pupils to appreciate the beauty and power of clear and artistic expression of thought and feeling; but this aim must be specific according to the nature of the selection to be taught. Some specific aims may be given as suggestive:

1. To appeal suitably to such instinctive tastes and interests of childhood as are already awake and active; for example, Second Reader, p. 3, *My Shadow;* p. 185, *A Visit from St. Nicholas;* p. 125, *Little Gustava;* p. 215, *The Children's Hour.*

2. To awaken and develop interests and tastes that are as yet dormant; for example, Second Reader, p. 42, *A Song for Little May;* p. 88, *The Brown Thrush.*

3. To develop and direct the imagination; for example, Second Reader, p. 72, *The New Moon;* p. 117, *Little Sorrow;* p. 45, *The Little Land;* p. 172, *The Wind.*

4. To arouse and quicken the sense of beauty; for example, Second Reader, p. 92, *Mother's World;* p. 155, *Lullaby.*

5. To exercise and cultivate the emotions; for example, Second Reader, p. 94, *Androclus and the Lion;* p. 135, *Ulysses;* p. 107, *A Night with a Wolf.*

6. To develop manners and morals through examples of character and conduct in action; for example, Second Reader, p. 114, *Joseph II and the Grenadier.*

7. To develop appreciation for the well-told story; for example, Second Reader, p. 5, *The Pail of Gold;* p. 12, *How I Turned the Grindstone;* p. 56, *The Blind Men and the Elephant;* p. 211, *How the Greeks Took Troy.*

8. To develop a true sense of humour; for example, Second Reader, p. 50, *Change About.*

9. To develop a sense of reverence; for example, Second Reader, p. 203, *The Lord is my Shepherd;* p. 218, *Abide With Me.*

GENERAL PRINCIPLES APPLICABLE IN THE TEACHING OF LITERATURE

There are four outstanding principles of general method that apply particularly in the teaching of Literature.

I. The pupil must, at the outset, be placed in a receptive attitude toward the lesson if the best results are to be secured. He must have some *purpose* in view if he is to be induced to concentrate his attention upon it. His purposes determine his interests, and hence the lesson must, in some way, be related to interests that already exist in his mind. Frequently his instinctive interest in action, in personality, or in excitement is sufficient incentive to secure his attention. A suspicion that a lesson contains a good story is often sufficient to ensure a careful reading of it, and a curiosity as to the writer's devices to make the story interesting will lead to a closer examination of it. But more frequently some special interest resulting from the time of year, the surroundings, or the work taken in some other subject, may be effectively utilized by the teacher. These interests of children are so numerous and so varied that there are few lessons in the Readers for which a receptive attitude of mind cannot be secured. It will be observed that the principle here enunciated corresponds to the "statement of the aim" in the Herbartian "Formal Steps".

II. The pupil's mind must be suitably prepared for the assimilation of the ideas contained in the lesson, by recalling old ideas and feelings that are related to those to be presented in the selection to be studied. He must be placed in a proper intellectual attitude to interpret the ideas and in a proper emotional attitude to appreciate the feelings. Neglect of the former may make the selection wholly meaningless to the pupil; neglect of the latter may result in entire indifference toward it. A proper intellectual attitude is necessary in any lesson, but in a lesson in grammar or arithmetic the emotional attitude may be almost completely absent. In literature, however, this emotional attitude is often of the greatest importance, and the neglect of it may mean an utter lack of appreciation of some literary masterpiece. This preparatory work may take the form of a recall of some of the common experiences of the pupil's life or a review of some facts taken, for instance, in a previous geography, history, or nature study lesson. The apperceptive power of the pupil's mind takes the new material of thought and feeling contained in the selection and weaves it into the web of his previous ideas and emotions.

III. The mind always proceeds from a vague and indistinct idea of a new presentation to a clear and defined idea of it. The process is always analytic-synthetic. In a literature lesson the order of procedure must be: (1) Let the pupil get that somewhat indistinct grasp of the thought and feeling which comes from a preliminary reading of it; (2) make this more definite by a process of analysis, by concentrating attention on the details; (3) make the idea completely definite by a clear grasp of the relations existing among the various details, that is, by a process of synthesis.

IV. No impression is complete without some form of expression. An idea or emotion is a very incomplete and useless thing until it is worked out in practice and conduct. The thoughts and feelings gained from the literature lesson must be given some kind of expression if they are to be fully realized. This expression may take many different forms. The pupils may merely read the selection, showing to the listeners their understanding and appreciation of it. If it is a story, they may reproduce it in their own words orally or in writing. They may sketch a scene or a situation with pencil, or with brush and colours. They may dramatize it, or act it in pantomime. They may create a story with a similar theme, or imitate a poem by a creation of their own. The expression may not be immediate but may be delayed for days or even years, and come in some modification of future conduct.

CHAPTER II

METHODS

IN JUNIOR FORMS

To introduce children to the world of literature, it is not necessary to wait until they have mastered the art of reading. The introduction should come long before they have learned to read, through listening to good stories told or read to them by others, through hearing suitable poems read or recited with spirit and feeling, and by memorizing nursery rhymes and gems of poetry.

The material to be used in primary grades has already been described. Early work in literature should be correlated with oral composition.

As to the comparative merits of reading and telling, much may be said on each side. In the early stages, telling must, of course, be the predominant if not the exclusive means of communicating the story. The matter and language can thus be better adjusted to the capacity of the individual pupil. The teacher who is familiar with the pupil's home life and surroundings has within his power a means of adapting the story to the attainments of the pupil that even the best writer of children's stories can hardly command. A situation in a story can frequently be made intelligible by reference to the pupil's own experience. Moreover, in telling the story, the teacher's gestures, facial expression, and tone of voice are likely to be more spontaneous and natural than would be the case in reading, and this gives immense assistance in interpreting aright the meaning and spirit of the selection.

Some teachers say that the incident, as in the case of Hawthorne's Tales, is so meagre and the language so exquisite, that the telling seems to be quite inadequate and inferior to the reading of the story. In such cases, variety may be afforded by reading, but generally speaking, it is more effective to tell the story.

The teacher should strive to become a good story-teller. This requires a good voice, animated gesture and facial expression, a good command of English words, power of graphic description and narration, restraint from digression and superfluous detail, and concentration of aim upon some definite point.

In teaching poetry to primary classes, the main object is to lead the pupils to feel the music and realize the imagery. To attain this end, the best beginning is made by a sympathetic and expressive rendering of the passage by the teacher. It can be recited many times incidentally, while he is asking the pupils to look at the pretty pictures suggested by the text. It is not necessary to enter at any length into an analysis of the poem, unless the pictures are arranged in an easy order, such as spring, summer, autumn, winter.

Memorization

One of the most valuable means of securing an appreciation of literature is the memorization of fine passages of prose and poetry. Pupils from the primary grades upward should be required to memorize systematically several lines of prose and poetry every week of the school year. During childhood the mind is at its most impressionable stage, and what is committed to memory is then retained longer and more accurately than what is memorized at any later period. The passages should be carefully selected and should be suited to the capacity and interests of the pupils. Nothing should be memorized that has not *some* meaning for them, but it would be impossible to require that every selection should be *fully* understood. The selections which children commit to memory in the most plastic period of their lives will often reveal a new and unexpected meaning and beauty in later years and will be a source of keen delight and satisfaction. The passages memorized will form a standard, unconscious it may be, by which to test the excellence of other selections.

It is of the greatest importance that the passages chosen should have artistic excellence in thought, feeling, music, imagery, and language. Moreover, these qualities must be present in such a form that they will, when properly presented by the teacher's reading or reciting, appeal, in some considerable measure, to the pupils' capacities and interests. Since there are so many noble passages in English literature, nothing of doubtful value should be memorized.

It is also very important that the teacher himself should have committed to memory and be able to recite freely and expressively every selection he requires his pupils to memorize. It is clear that, if he has memorized it himself, the pupils will be more likely to feel it worth while to do the same.

In conducting a lesson in memorization, it is well for the teacher to arouse the interest of the pupils in the selection as a whole by reciting it himself with expression. Next, he should see that the pupils understand as clearly as possible the meaning, and realize and appreciate, as far as they are able, the feeling of the passage. It should be treated first as an ordinary literature lesson, after the manner already described. It should then be read aloud several times by individual pupils, all trying meanwhile to commit it to memory by concentration of attention on the ideas and their relations, the words and their meanings. The principles of all habit formation apply here—attention to the thing to be learned, so as to get a clear understanding of it, and then repetition with attention. When it has been read several times, individual pupils should be asked to recite it without any aid. It will be found more satisfactory to memorize a complete stanza at a time, or at least a part that expresses a complete thought, rather than to commit to memory a line at a time. With young pupils, however, it is well to take small units and let the children repeat one or two lines at a time till they can give the whole stanza with ease and accuracy.

It is important that all repetition should be individual, not simultaneous.

Where the latter method is in use, it is noticeable that pupils adopt a uniform tone and measured rhythm, both of which are undesirable. Moreover, especially with young pupils, there is a danger that absurd blunders made by individuals may pass unnoticed, because the teacher has not the opportunity of detecting them. When the passage has been memorized, it should be repeated daily for a time and then repeated at longer intervals, until there is little probability of its being forgotten.

IN SENIOR FORMS

The Teacher's Preparation

The teacher must make himself thoroughly acquainted with the lesson that he has to teach. When it is an extract, he should be familiar with the longer work from which it is taken. He cannot teach the lesson "Maggie Tulliver" with the highest appreciation if he has not read *The Mill on the Floss*. But there is more than mere information required for successful teaching. In poetry the teacher should feel delight in the music, the expression, the emotion, till he is eager to communicate his feelings to the pupils. This enthusiasm, however, should not have in it any insincerity, or extravagant commendation of the poem or the author. The teacher who has wide information and genuine interest in his work will seldom fail to arouse a real pleasure in the literature lesson.

The relationship between the teacher and the pupils must be cordial if the lesson is to be successful. This is true in any subject, but the sympathetic bond must be especially strong in the literature lesson.

Preparation of Pupils

It has already been pointed out that it is frequently necessary to give preliminary lessons in nature study, science, history, or geography before the lesson in literature is presented. The pupil must have the right information before the literature lesson can arouse the emotion that the author wishes him to feel.

Not only is the possession of the right information necessary, but the pupil should be in the right mood for the lesson. A class that has just returned to the room after the games at recess is not in the proper state of mind to appreciate, at once, the recitation by the teacher of,

> Break, break, break,
> On thy cold gray stones, O sea!

Even the enthusiasm and scholarship of the teacher will fail to be effective under these circumstances. He should arouse in the pupils the proper mental and emotional state by a very short talk on friendship. He can refer to the well-known stories of David and Jonathan, or Damon and Pythias, and tell them of the friendship existing between Arthur Hallam and Alfred Tennyson.

Before studying *Lead, Kindly Light* (p. 315, Third Reader) the teacher might ask the pupils to picture a solitary traveller in the desert far from home. Night is approaching; the darkness gathers, and the air grows chill. What would be the nature of his feelings? Away in the distance he discovers a faint light glimmering as from a lantern. Now, how would he feel? Continue till the pupils can see each part of the picture, the spiritual significance of which they are to learn through the poem.

To give an extended account of the author's life is a poor introduction, unless there is something of unusual interest about his personality or achievements. The pupils usually do not know anything about him, and the teacher's aim, in this preparatory work, is to relate the thought and feeling of the poem to the properly assimilated knowledge and experience of the pupils. In some cases, they may have made a favourable acquaintance with the author in another poem, and this may give the necessary stimulus to their interest in his life. The best time, however, to give a biography of an author, when that is helpful, is after the lesson has been studied, for then the pupils will appreciate what the teacher has to say about him personally.

In some poems, the circumstances under which they are written will be the only introduction necessary, as in the case of *Break, break, break* or *The Recessional.*

There is often an appropriate time for the teaching of a literature lesson. Sometimes it is the season of the year. The lesson on *An Apple Orchard in the Spring* should come when the blossoms are stimulating every bird and child with their loveliness, fragrance, and promise. *The First Ploughing* and the various poems on birds and flowers should come at this season. They can be followed, in turn, by *A Midsummer Song* and *The Maple*. There are poems in the Readers for September, November, Indian Summer, and Winter; and a wealth of material for the Christmas season. Yet the season may not always determine the time for such lessons. The pupil who has observed again and again an apple orchard in the spring, and who knows birds and trees, has a store of memories that will enable him to picture vividly what he reads about these at any time.

It may be objected that these methods of introduction make the pupil depend too much on the teacher, and do not throw him sufficiently on his own resources. It is to be remembered, however, that the great object of teaching literature is to cultivate a taste for it. When the pupil approaches a selection with ideas and feelings which are already, in his consciousness, related to those presented in the poem, he is in the best possible mental attitude to appreciate it, and the probability of his liking it is much greater than if it were presented without any such introduction. The pupil's first impressions of a poem are all-important, and it is essential that his first introduction to it should be made under the most favourable circumstances. If his first acquaintance with poetry is made under pleasant conditions, he will inevitably develop a taste for poetical literature, and that is the object which the teacher has in view. When this taste has been formed, it will not be necessary that the teacher should be at hand in order to recall the proper experiences for the interpretation of a passage. The pupil will read appreciatively on his own account, without any such assistance.

In all cases, the preparation of the pupils for the lesson must be short. Nothing more should be given than will suffice to bring them into a suitable mood; usually some simple experience of their lives is ample. The time for the lesson is always limited, and the proportion between the introduction and the main theme must always be maintained.

Presentation

The next step in the development of the lesson is the presentation. How shall this be done? There are three ways: The teacher may ask the pupils to read the lesson silently at their seats or at home and come prepared to participate in the discussion; or he may ask some of them to read the lesson aloud; or he, himself, may read it to the pupils. The merits of each of these methods will be considered.

In prose, it is advisable to let the pupils read the selection before the lesson is taken up by the teacher. The pupils must have practice in getting the thought from the symbols on the printed page and in grasping the general trend of the story, the description, or the argument. The work will be mainly intellectual, but the pupils may also, at this stage, have practice in discovering the emotional elements in some of the prose extracts.

In the higher Forms, the teacher may occasionally allow some of his best readers to read a poem aloud, where the emotion is evident or the narrative plain. *The Barefoot Boy*, p. 118, Fourth Reader; *The Homes of England*, p. 375; and *Bernardo del Carpio*, p. 131, are examples of this kind.

It is usually a better plan for the teacher to read the poem to the pupils. With many poems of exquisite music and imagery, such as *The Bugle Song*, p. 337, Third Reader, the reading by a pupil who has not yet caught the meaning and spirit will be a failure, and the teacher will see that the mood that he has prepared with care at the opening is so certain to be dissipated that he must intervene in order to prevent the spoiling of the lesson. But the teacher who has studied the poem and whose feelings have been deeply stirred by its music and pictures can, through his reading, communicate to his pupils his own appreciation; and it will be a dull pupil who does not feel the contagion. It is, however, not well to insist on too great uniformity in method; the spirit rather than the form is vital.

Value of Oral Reading in the Interpretation and Appreciation of Literature

1. To the reader himself. Poetical literature is akin to music. Poetry was originally sung by the minstrel, and the thought and feeling were communicated to the audience solely by the ear. The study of poetry by the eye is artificial, modern, and contrary to our hereditary instincts. We should not argue that the best way to appreciate music is found in following the symbols on the music sheet. It is only the highly educated musician who can imagine the delights of music by an examination of the written text. To some degree, it is the same with poetry. The music of the words and the appropriateness of the rhythm cannot be fully perceived by merely silent reading. The eye alone would never detect the exquisite music of such a poem as *Hide and Seek*, Third Reader, p. 50, or *Break, break, break*, p. 201. Nor could it perceive the suitability of the rhythm to the theme, as exhibited in *How*

They Brought the Good News from Ghent to Aix, Fourth Reader, p. 351. In this poem, we can hear in the rhythm the hoof beats of the horses as they gallop along. How often have we felt a new meaning and appropriateness that our voice alone has suggested!

2. To the listeners. The contagious nature of emotion has already been pointed out. The good reader, by his sympathetic and expressive rendering of the poem, may reveal to his listeners depths of feeling, the existence of which they had not before suspected. We have often been thrilled by a new emotion, upon hearing a familiar passage read by another.

Every teacher should be a good reader. His tone of voice, his movement, his gestures are the signs by which the pupils interpret his emotional attitude. If he is not already a good reader, he should bend all his energies to become one. Persevering practice, attention to mechanical features, such as distinct articulation, pausing, flexibility of voice, and, above all, a sympathetic appreciation of the author's thought and feeling, will soon convert a poor reader into a good one. He will soon find that his voice will accommodate itself insensibly in pitch, tone, and movement to the changing emotions of the poem. The delight of the lesson will be greatly enhanced where the reader lends to the rhyme of the poet the music of his voice.

The reading reveals the general thought of the poem. In simpler poems, the pupils will recognize in the reading the relationship and the intent of many of the subordinate parts. But the intellectual side is only secondary. Literature, in its finer forms, is not primarily an intellectual subject, such as grammar or mathematics. The emotional tone, the spiritual meaning, and the artistic form—these are the main elements, and these can be best developed by good reading. The teacher should acquire the habit of reading poetry aloud in his home, and should induce his pupils to follow his example. Further, as two senses will give a more vivid realization of thought than one, the pupil, in the class, should follow with his eye the reading of the teacher; and it is helpful for a church congregation to follow with the eye the reading of the scripture lesson by the minister.

The Development of the Main Thought

The teacher should next assist the pupils to discover the main thought of the lesson. In many cases the meaning will be very vague, and the pupils will have difficulty in formulating a terse and comprehensive statement of the subject of the poem. If the question is asked in a stereotyped form, such as "What is the main thought of the poem?" the enthusiasm of the pupils is often chilled. The teacher may, if it is a narrative poem, ask for the main points in the story, and may assist the pupils by calling attention to some pertinent passage, or by removing difficulties by means of questions or explanations. In all cases, it is well to accept a partially correct answer by the pupils, and to try to improve its imperfection by questioning, until a fairly complete and substantial statement has been given. Every answer which contains even a fragment of sound thought should receive due recognition. In some cases it is sufficient, at the outset, to take an imperfect statement of the main thought, since the study of the poem will reveal its defects.

The teacher must keep before his pupils this statement, so that at the conclusion of the lesson they will be quite ready to replace it by a more accurate one. The teacher should be careful that the emotions aroused by the poem are not unduly weakened or dissipated by the analysis of its intellectual content. Many lessons by young teachers fail just at this point, by reason of questioning unskilfully or by rejecting answers that do not correspond to their own cut-and-dried preconceptions.

The teacher should follow a similar method in discovering the leading thought of the subdivisions of the poem. These often correspond to the stanza forms, but the lesson may become very wearisome by insisting on too great detail. The poem often falls into two or three main divisions, into which the various stanzas may be grouped. With Senior Forms it is a good exercise to ask the pupils to make this grouping, but, with those not so advanced, the teacher himself may make it and ask the pupils for the central thought in each group. In the teacher's anxiety to have these subjects clearly stated, he runs the risk of wasting time and, worse than that, of killing whatever interest the pupils may have had up to this point. If the pupils could give these subjects with perfect clearness now, there would be little else to do. The greatest care must be exercised to prevent the work becoming mechanical, thus destroying the interest and making the selection distasteful.

With some pupils, the logical sense is quite strong, and they find their greatest delight in seeing the purpose of each part in a complex mechanism. With others, this work does not afford much pleasure. These are children who, later, can take delight in the flimsy plot of a musical comedy. Such pupils should be encouraged to do their best to discover some points of beauty or skill in the arrangement of the selection. In different lessons there is a difference in construction. In some, the logical connection and development is so important that this quality must be stressed, but the works of some authors have merits which throw the arrangement into a very subordinate position; for example, "Ring out, Wild Bells", from *In Memoriam*.

Minute Analysis

The next stage in the analysis is the examination of the passage minutely. There is always a place in the lesson for the study of words and phrases. The teacher should ask questions on these, in order to ascertain if the pupils have felt their force and vitality. They are to be taken up only to illuminate and impress the main thoughts and emotions of the poem.

In some cases, as in prose lessons, the pupils may acquire the dictionary habit. This develops and cultivates a studious disposition and accuracy of statement. But in poetry there are many subtle meanings that the dictionary will not give, but which the pupil has learned through contact with educated people and acquaintance with books. Most of the words that people use have not been learned from the dictionary, but from their context in reading or conversation.

On the other hand, many lessons are spoiled by too constant inquiry into meanings. There is much mere learning of meanings without reference to the thought or emotion that they are intended to explain. Many words are explained that are already understood. The fault may be due to the teacher's experience with annotated text-books of literature. The teacher, who has been prepared for his examination by this method, is disposed to carry it into Elementary School work, till even *The Recessional* becomes merely a theme for learning verbal meanings.

Allusions

There are many references in the text-books to geographical, scientific, and historical matters. If these allusions. In poems such as *The Armada* there must be a preliminary lesson such as has been indicated. Very often the enthusiast in these subjects will make literature a mere peg on which to hang much information. Teachers often make long digressions in connection with these allusions, till the mood of the poem is completely lost in the mist of the disquisitions. The same method should be adopted in teaching allusions as in teaching the meanings of words. Only such explanation is necessary as will show the purpose of the author in introducing the allusions. In poems such as *The Armada* there must be considerable explanation given, before the pupils will feel the emotion that the author hopes to kindle by the mention of the names that are used in it. With Canadian children, the effect in the case of this poem cannot be so great as with English children, who are more familiar with the special geographical and historical associations.

The teacher of young people cannot hope, by explanation of the allusions, to arouse all the pleasure and the vitality of emotion that will be induced in the reader who has the culture that comes of wide reading; nor can the teacher communicate this emotion when the information is new. The pleasure comes, later on, from the recall of information that was assimilated in earlier years.

The Imagery

The language of poetry is generally concrete. The artist may wish to give expression to a general truth, or philosophical principle, or ethereal fancy. These appear very abstract, but the artist embodies in material forms the idea he wishes to convey. The poet expresses his thought by the suggestion of material imagery, and emotion is most readily aroused by these images.

Antony, in his funeral oration after Cæsar's death, knew how to arouse his audience to fury by showing them Cæsar's wounds and holding before them Cæsar's mantle with its rents. Not always can the real object be produced for these emotional effects, but the teacher can sometimes bring into the class-room, for the benefit of young pupils, concrete material such as pictures and work in manual training. He can also call attention, at times, to the falling snow or the colour of the leaves or the sky, by asking the pupils to look out of the class-room windows. But in most cases, he has to be content with trying to recall the memory of these natural things. This shows how valuable has been the excursion of the boy into the country, and his experience on holidays by the river and in the harvest field. The nature study lesson furnishes the material for future enjoyment of poetry.

The pupils in our schools are very capable in realizing visual imagery. They can see the visual image very readily with its colour, form, and movement. They can arrange the objects in the picture with foreground, background, light, and shade.

But it is quite a different matter when they try to realize auditory imagery. In the poem *Waterloo,* Fourth Reader, p. 311, they can see the picture in "bright the lamps shone o'er fair women and brave men". They see the large ball-room with its glass chandeliers, the costumes of handsome ladies, the scarlet uniforms and the decorations of the officers and the nobility. But can they realize the next imagery, that of sound, "and when music arose with its voluptuous swell"? Do they hear the squeaking of one or two fiddles or do they hear the voluminous sound of regimental bands? Do they notice the varying metre from the stately iambic to the sudden "voluptuous swell" of the foot of three syllables in waltz time?

These images of sight and sound picture the gaiety and magnificence of this festive scene, in order to make more marked the contrast with the fear and pathos of the farewells. This contrast is enforced by the two auditory images:

> And all went merry as a marriage bell;
> But hush! hark! a deep sound strikes like a rising knell!

Can your pupils image the wedding-bells chiming from the cathedral some afternoon in June, when suddenly the ear catches the sound of a death-bell tolling from another church? Any reader who cannot realize the sounds of those two bells with their discordant effects will miss the intention of Byron.

The pupils, through the stimulation of their senses, must have experienced the luxurious effects of orchards, flower gardens, and clover fields; the odours of apple blossoms and the smell and taste of the "full-juiced apple waxing over-mellow"; the perfumes and temperatures of spring, midsummer, and winter if they are to read nature literature intelligently and feel its charm. The words must have meaning if they are to awaken the feeling that was part of the original experience.

The Literature of Noble Thought

In literature, as in other arts, there is a great deal that is merely decorative. It is not the purpose here to disparage this form of art. "A thing of beauty is a joy for ever. Its loveliness increases." Some of the most famous portraits and landscapes in the picture galleries afford infinite pleasure to the student of art by the technique in colour, drawing, and arrangement. They are greater than photography. "The light that never was on sea or land, the consecration and the poet's dream" have given them a beauty that is greater than the realism of the actual person or natural scene. It is the same in literature. The author's feelings, his language, the rhythm of his words, and his delicate fancy afford the reader greater delight than he has ever known when he has met similar persons, scenes, or actions in real life. This is genuine æsthetic pleasure, similar to the pleasure that people derive from china, music, or landscape gardening.

There is, however, a higher form of art in both pictures and literature. There are pictures that suggest some noble aspiration, some great universal truth, some great conflict between duty and interest. We feel instinctively that these are greater than pictures possessing mere masterly technique. It is the same in literature.

There are poems in which we feel that the thoughts and feelings are sublime. Perhaps the technique of these is not equal to that of the poetry described in the preceding paragraph, but the experienced teacher has felt his pupils lifted above mundane affairs, when they begin to grasp the true significance of such poems. The youngest pupils show their appreciation by wide open eyes, when these are read. They instinctively feel that this work is better than the merely pretty and dainty things in poetry.

In the *Ontario Readers* we have numerous poems of this nature. In the First Reader, the pupils instinctively feel that *Piping Down the Valleys Wild* is of different calibre from *Three Little Kittens*. *The Lord is my Shepherd*, *Lead, Kindly Light*, and *To a Waterfowl*, are examples of this class.

In teaching these lessons, the spiritual meaning should be constantly emphasized.

The mere statement of the thought is not impressive. It is the presentation of it in poetical form that makes its effect impressive and lasting. The pupils may be led to discover how the author has accomplished this by means of the concrete embodiment of imagery, language, metaphor, and music.

Recapitulation

The lesson is often dropped just at this time, leaving an impression somewhat like that of a science room, with the petals and leaves on the desks and the floor, after the class in botany has been dismissed. No act of analysis is complete without a final synthesis. The examination of the various phases of the whole must be followed by a reconstruction in which are perceived the relations of the various phases to each other and to the unity of the whole. These various parts must be closely related to one another if the final conception of the poem is to be definite. When the analysis is in progress, the teacher should not, of course, take each part by itself and examine it as if it were an isolated thing, but its relation to what has gone before should be more or less clearly perceived. When the analysis is complete, there should be a final synthesis in which the relations of the various parts stand out definitely. This can be done by means of a statement of the main thought in concise but comprehensive terms. If the teacher has accepted an imperfect statement at the beginning, the pupils will now be in a position to discover its inadequacy and supply the part that is lacking. Then the subjects of the various subdivisions or stanzas can be restated in suitable terms that will show the proper relationships. This reconstruction may also take the form of oral or written reproduction of the selection. This is especially valuable after the prose lessons. There should follow an oral reading of the passage by the pupils, which will serve to show the teacher how much of the feeling of the poem has been absorbed, how clearly the pupils have understood the meaning, and what misconceptions have arisen in their minds.

Mistakes in Teaching Literature

There are some mistakes in teaching literature that are noted here, in order that they may be avoided:

1. Teaching pupils about literature, instead of teaching literature itself; for example, teaching biography, etymology, history, geography, or science in the literature lesson, because some feature of one or more of these may be suggested by the language of the lesson. A knowledge of such subjects is merely preparatory to the study of literature itself.

2. Teaching merely the meanings of words and phrases, and omitting the greater things of imagery, thought, beauty of language, and the spirit of the writer.

3. Trying to force appreciation by telling the pupils they must learn to like such and such works because educated people like them. It is useless, at this time, to try to develop the critical spirit, as the pupil has not a sufficiently wide acquaintance with literary works on which to form a judgment.

4. Doing for the pupil what he should be led to do for himself. A literature lesson, in which the teacher has been doing all the talking, or both asking and answering questions, will be barren of good results.

5. Paraphrasing. Short passages may be paraphrased, in order to show whether the pupil has understood the force and vitality of the metaphor or the condensed expression. But paraphrasing must be used with great discretion. The teacher will not make the pupils appreciate the beauty of a fine literary selection by converting refined gold into low grade ore.

6. Attempting to draw some moral from every lesson. Not all lessons are didactic. If the pupils have sympathized with what is noble and just in the story, the statement of a moral at the conclusion is unnecessary. Yet in poems that are plainly didactic, for example, *To a Waterfowl*, Fourth Reader, p. 377, the moral lesson must occupy the first place. There the teacher should show how the author has enforced the lesson of *confidence in God's guidance* by the incident of the migrating waterfowl, the imagery, the music, the arrangement of parts, and the similarity of his own position to that of the bird.

7. Dwelling unnecessarily on the intellectual side of a poem that is mainly emotional and musical; for example, *The Bugle Song*, Third Reader, p. 337, and *The Solitary Reaper*, Fourth Reader, p. 261. In the former case, the pupils should be led to realize the visual imagery, should hear, in imagination, the bugle calls and fading echoes, and enjoy the rare and appropriate music. In the second case, the teacher should call attention to the artistic suggestions of loneliness, distance, antiquity, sadness, and vagueness that are suggested by "old, unhappy, far-off things, and battles long ago", and by such possible situations of English travellers in remote parts of the world, and should show that these elements are suitable for the circumstances under which the poet sees the girl. He who questions merely to find out the meaning of the poem, the relation to that of its subordinate parts, and the meaning of the words and phrases, is using a very heavy tool on a very delicate mechanism. Such works must be treated deftly and lightly.

Extensive Reading

The class of literature that we have described in the preceding methods is condensed literature, where thought is large in proportion to the number of the words. It must be read by a process of close thinking, in an analytic, exhaustive manner. There must be a clear comprehension of the central ideas, and a strong grasp of minor thoughts or details, and the relation of these to the central ideas. While this power to grasp thought intensively is very valuable, we should also have the power to grasp the thought rapidly and comprehensively.

In some works, the thought is not so condensed and confined. Here, the main effort of the reader is to grasp the thoughts successively in a rapid, clear, and comprehensive manner. He must be able to read a book chapter by chapter and grasp the central ideas, to hold paragraph after paragraph, chapter after chapter, in his consciousness, so that each gives added illumination to the main thought and, at the end, the whole of the work stands out in its entirety. He must learn to grasp the central thought in each section as he proceeds—to sift the wheat from the chaff. The minor details have been of value in giving him the main thought, but the real ability of the good reader consists in dropping these minor details from the mind and holding steadily on to the more important facts.

This method gives a greater power of sustained attention and a wider acquaintance with good literature. Most of our reading is done in this way. It would be impossible otherwise to get a wide range, as time does not permit of minute analysis, and many of our longer works are so diffuse that they would not repay such careful study.

The supplementary, or extensive, reading may be given as seat work or home work. As seat work, it can come as a grateful relief from the arduous tasks in the ungraded school and will keep many an active mind from getting into mischief. By questioning about the main facts the teacher can assure himself that the work has actually been done. This questioning should not be used only to catch the negligent; it should give pleasure to the pupils as a conversation with them about their pleasant occupation. It should be done very informally, often as two intelligent people would discuss a book. The questions should be broad in their scope and should not dwell on matters of detail. If it is a story that is to be considered, it should be examined as follows: Discover what are the difficulties set up; how they are brought about; how they are overcome; how many threads of interest there are; why certain characters are introduced; what would be the effect if certain parts were omitted; to what extent the final solution is logical.

When the examination is finished, a series of compositions might be written on topics connected with the story. For instance, if *Rip Van Winkle* has been studied, a series of three compositions might be assigned: (1) Rip's domestic life; (2) his adventure in the mountain; (3) his return to the village. Three compositions would be better than a single one on the whole story, because too great condensation usually detracts from the value, and because the excellence of a school composition is usually in inverse proportion to its length.

It is exceedingly important that the teacher should see that these written exercises are not made distasteful to the pupil. They are very valuable if they are not considered irksome. The object is not so much to give skill in composition as to create a taste for wide and excellent reading. It would be better to allow this written reproduction to drop rather than to associate the pleasures of literature with something disagreeable.

CHAPTER III

ILLUSTRATIVE LESSONS

In the lessons that follow, the answers given to questions are those which pupils may be expected to give after corrections and additions have been made by themselves and the teacher.

Professor Alexander has said:

> It is impossible to exemplify on paper actual teaching. Actual teaching, as all other practical matters, is in large measure determined by circumstances and conditions which are never twice the same. A large part of a teacher's skill lies in the sympathetic perception of these conditions and in the power of adapting himself to them on the spur of the moment. The teacher should have a definite aim in view, and a general conception of the proper method to be followed; but these will be modified by the character of the pupils before him, of the answers given, of the manifestation of interest, and the comprehension of the various points brought forward. A question quite proper in one case will be quite out of place in another. What knowledge should be imparted by the instructor, what elicited from the pupils themselves, what matters dwelt upon, what lightly passed over—these things can only be determined by the actual circumstances.

PANTOMIME

Little Miss Muffet

(Primer, page 75)

Little Miss Muffet sits on a low chair eating from an imaginary dish. The spider comes creeping softly behind her. When he reaches her side, he sits quietly down. Then she sees him and, in a great fright, jumps up and runs away.

DRAMATIZATION

Little Boy Blue

(Primer, page 68)

The senior division of the primary class had read the story of Little Boy Blue.

Norman asked: "May we play it? May I be Little Boy Blue?"

Allan said: "I'd like to be the farmer".

Dorothy wished to be the farmer's wife.

Clara asked if the pupils of the highest class might be the cows and the sheep.

As Norman was enthusiastic and eager to express himself, he was permitted to direct the movements of the different characters.

The farmer selected a horse and prepared to take him to market, while Little Boy Blue could be seen tramping along the road (the front part of the room). The cows and sheep were grazing quietly near by.

As Little Boy Blue approached the farmer, he removed his cap and said: "Good morning, sir, do you want a boy?"

Farmer: "Yes, I want one to watch the cows and the sheep."

Little Boy Blue: "I can do that, sir."

Farmer (handing Little Boy Blue a toy horn that had been brought to school for use during a drawing lesson): "Here is a horn, then. If they try to go away, blow this, and they will come back."

Little Boy Blue: "I will, sir."

The farmer drove away, and Little Boy Blue watched the cows and the sheep. Once they were about to wander away (among the aisles), but Little Boy Blue blew the horn, and they immediately returned. He soon grew tired of watching them; they seemed to be content to graze quietly where they were. He leaned against a haystack (a chair) and fell asleep. The cows were soon in the corn and the sheep in the meadow, where the farmer saw them as he was driving home. But he could not see Little Boy Blue. He called:

Little Boy Blue,
Come blow your horn,
The sheep are in the meadow,
The cows are in the corn.

Farmer: "Wife, where is Little Boy Blue?"

Wife: "He is under the haystack, fast asleep."

Farmer (going to haystack):

Little Boy Blue,
Come blow your horn.

The boy jumped up, blew a blast on the horn, and the sheep and cows immediately came back.

Little Boy Blue: "It was my fault and I'm sorry."

Farmer: "All right, you'll take better care of them next time."

The Story of Henny Penny

(Primer, page 48)

When the teacher suggests that a game be played, many pupils fairly project themselves backward in an effort to look so well that they may be chosen to take part in it.

The teacher wrote "Dorothy" on the black-board. Dorothy whispered that she would like to play the story of Henny Penny. (The adventures of Henny Penny had been recounted the day before.) The teacher wrote the story of Henny Penny. As Dorothy had sufficient self-confidence and a good memory, she was allowed to choose her part, which was certain to be that of the principal character. Had she not possessed these qualities, she would have been assigned a minor part during the first attempt at dramatizing this story. The teacher wrote "Rooster Pooster" on the black-board. "I should like to be Rooster Pooster", said Albert. "Turkey Lurkey", wrote the teacher. "I'd like to be Turkey Lurkey", said another. In this or some similar way, the parts were assigned.

As the play began, Henny Penny was discovered pecking at imaginary worms in the garden; suddenly she jumped up in a great fright. "Oh, the sky is falling!" she said, "I must run and tell the king". She ran down the road (an aisle) till she met Rooster Pooster.

When he saw her coming, he stopped crowing and asked, "Where are you going, Henny Penny?" "Oh", she said, "the sky is falling, and I am going to tell the king". "I will go too", said Rooster Pooster. They ran down the road till they met Turkey Lurkey gobbling contentedly. The usual formula was repeated, and Turkey Lurkey ran on with them.

But the fox (villain) was waiting around the corner. "Where are you going, Henny Penny, Rooster Pooster, and Turkey Lurkey?" said he. "Oh, Fox Lox", they said, "the sky is falling and we are going to tell the king". "I will show you the way." "Oh, no, Fox Lox, we know you. We will not go with you."

So they ran and ran, but had to return home because they did not find the king's house.

Wishes

(Primer, page 52)

The pupils knew by the pictures on page 52 that the lesson would be a delightful one, but when they attempted to read it, they found difficulties that lessened their pleasure somewhat.

They enjoyed reading "I wish I could find a little fat fly", but "sad little sigh" and "an odd little shrug" were very difficult to say and were meaningless until the children imitated the teacher's "sad little sighs" and "odd little shrugs".

The pupils were then asked which little chicken they would like to be. The first pupil to respond was chosen. He went to the front of the room, which was then a garden, and with a much bigger sigh than was necessary, complained: "I wish I could find a little fat fly".

The other pupils then eagerly studied the page, that they might learn what the next little chicken said and did. The teacher was always ready to tell them any words they could not discover for themselves. One pupil could make a shrug but could not remember the second little chicken's words, so another was found who could say what the second little chicken said in just the way he would say it if he could talk. The other little chickens and the mother hen were chosen in a similar manner.

The mother hen could be seen busily scratching at one end of the garden, while her little chickens were walking aimlessly about.

First Chicken (after sighing):

"I wish I could find a little fat fly."

Second Chicken (with a shrug):

"I wish I could find a fat little bug."

Third Chicken (with a squeaky voice):

"I wish I could feel some corn in my beak."

Fourth Chicken (sighing):

"I wish I could find a fat worm on a leaf."

Mother Hen (impatiently):

"See here, if you want things to eat, just come here and scratch."

Indian Lullaby

Rock-a-bye, my little owlet,
In the mossy, swaying nest,
With thy little woodland brothers,
Close thine eyes and take thy rest.

Hush-a-bye, my little owlet,
Many voices sing to thee;
"Hush-a-bye," the water whispers,
"Hush!" replies the tall pine tree.—LONGFELLOW

There had been language lessons on the habits of the Indians; their way of living had been worked out, as far as possible, on the sand-table, and pictures representing Indian life had been shown. The pupils had eagerly constructed an Indian home—"Dark behind it rose the forest" (twigs from the pine and other evergreen trees), "Bright before it beat the water".

The lessons in drawing, painting, end modelling had been connected with this work. From their boxes of coloured crayons, the pupils had selected the colours used in making the pine trees, the grass, the bark of the trees, the owl in the tree, the wigwams, etc.

From the many beautiful Indian lullabies that would have been suitable, the teacher selected the *Indian Lullaby* by Longfellow. During the periods set apart for music, the pupils had been taught the desired melody with the syllable "loo".

Teacher. "How does your mother put baby to sleep?"

Pupils. "My mother rocks the baby in her arms." "Mine puts him on the bed and he falls asleep." "We rock our baby in a cradle," etc.

Teacher. "The picture I give you will show you what the Indian mother does with her baby."

Each pupil was given a small picture showing an Indian baby in his cradle suspended from a tree. These pictures had been cut from a supplement to *Primary Education*.

Teacher. "What has the mother done?"

Pupils. "She has put her baby in a basket and hung it on a tree."

Teacher. "Is the baby in the picture awake or asleep?"

Pupils. "He is asleep."

Teacher. "What could the baby see before he went to sleep?"

Here a picture—fourteen by twenty inches—was shown. It was a good representation of an Indian home and its surroundings. The pupils had made use of this picture when working at the sand-table.

Pupils. "He could see the pine trees, the water, the wigwams, the canoes, the Indians," etc.

Teacher. "What could the baby hear while swinging in his cradle?"

Pupils. "He could hear the Indians talking. He could hear the wind among the trees; the water; the birds singing in the woods; the cry of an owl; perhaps wolves, bears," etc.

Teacher. "What other babies lived in the woods?"

Pupils. "Birds, squirrels, owls, wolves," etc.

Teacher. "A man once wrote what he thought an Indian mother might have sung to her baby. This is what he thought she would sing." (The teacher recited the *Indian Lullaby*.)

Individual pupils then repeated one stanza at a time with the assistance of the teacher.

The pupils sang softly the melody they had learned to "loo"; then all tried to sing the words with the teacher. The purpose was to emphasize the rhythm and interpret the spirit of the poem. The lesson occupied twelve to fifteen minutes. At another time, hectographed copies of the poem were given to the pupils, and as they had already partly memorized it, they soon learned to read it.

CHAPTER IV
FORM I: SENIOR GRADE
ILLUSTRATIVE LESSONS

THE WIND AND THE LEAVES

(First Reader, page 49)

It is the aim of this lesson to help the pupils to appreciate imaginative descriptions of some natural phenomena. This lesson will be best appreciated if taken some day in autumn when the leaves are falling. If the pupils have recently noticed the wind rushing through the trees, scattering the many-coloured leaves and driving them before it along the ground, they will be in the best mood to enter into the spirit of the poem.

What is the time of the year that the poem speaks about? The autumn.

Select all the things that tell you this. The leaves have "dresses of red and gold"; "summer is gone"; "the days grow cold"; the leaves come "fluttering" down; the "fields" are "brown".

What did the wind mean by "Come o'er the meadows with me, and play"? It meant that they should come down from the trees and be blown away by the wind across the fields.

What does it mean by "Put on your dresses of red and gold"? Before they fall, the leaves have many beautiful colours.

What was the colour of their dresses in summer? When do they begin to change colour very quickly?

What leaves show the most beautiful colours? What different colours have you noticed that leaves have?

When does the wind call? When it blows loudly or whistles.

Do you know what the wind says when it calls? Why not? We do not understand the language that it speaks.

How did the leaves show that they understood? They obeyed at once and came down from the trees.

What is meant by "fluttering" down? They came down slowly, moving from side to side, and turning over and over as they fell. (This could be shown in the class-room quite easily.)

Which line in the first stanza corresponds in meaning with the third line of the second? The second line.

What makes the fields "brown"? It is the end of the summer, and the grass and the plants have dried up.

What colours have the fields at other seasons of the year? Green in the spring, golden in the summer, white in the winter.

What are "the soft little songs" of the leaves? The rustling sounds they make as they are blown about by the wind.

Why do we not understand their songs? For the same reason that we do not understand the call of the wind—their language is not ours.

"Winter had called them." What is the voice of winter? The cold winds that roar and whistle.

What is meant by "content"? The leaves were quite glad to answer the call.

Why were they content? The work that they had been doing all summer long was done; they were tired and sleepy and glad to go to bed.

When may it be said that the leaves are "fast asleep"? When they lie quietly on the ground, no longer blown about by the wind.

How were they kept warm during their long sleep? The snow came and covered them up warmly, like a "blanket".

What does the whole lesson describe? The falling of the leaves.

What does the first stanza speak of? The call of the wind.

The second? The answer of the leaves.

The third? The leaves asleep.

Tell the story of the poem in your own words.

PIPING DOWN THE VALLEYS WILD

(First Reader, page 52)

AIM

To enable the pupils to appreciate the pretty pictures and the music, and to learn how their pretty songs were written.

PREPARATION

In far-away countries there are many sheep, and they require shepherds. These shepherds, as they can rest while their sheep feed, sometimes amuse themselves by cutting oat straws and making them into little flutes. They cut holes in the straws, just as you see holes in flutes or in tin whistles. They learn to play very pretty tunes. David, king of Israel, was, in his youth, a shepherd boy, and he learned to play beautiful music while he watched his sheep. The Psalms that you find in the Bible were composed by him.

PRESENTATION

Now let us read about a shepherd who was playing music. (The teacher reads the poem.) While he was playing, what did he see? He saw a little child sitting on a cloud.

What was the child doing? He was laughing.

Why? He liked the music.

What kind of music was it? It was pleasant, full of joy.

Where was the shepherd? In a valley.

Tell what the valley was like. It was wild. It had big rocks and hills on each side, and a cloud was over the valley.

What did the child ask him to do? To play "a song about a Lamb".

Why did he do that? Because the sheep were pretty and he thought he should like to hear pretty music about them.

How did the child like it? He asked the shepherd to play the tune again, and it was such beautiful music that the keen enjoyment of it made the tears come to his eyes.

What did the child next ask? He wished to have the music put into words, so he asked the shepherd to "sing" it.

How did the child enjoy it? It was so lovely that he "wept with joy".

What did he ask the shepherd to do? To "write" it down.

Why? The child thought it was so lovely that he wanted other children to hear it, too.

Yes, that is the way that we come to have all these pretty poems in our books. If they were only played or sung, not so many children could have the opportunity of enjoying them.

What do you need when you write? We need pens, and paper, and ink.

The shepherd had not steel pens, and white paper, and black ink. He may have used the bark of trees to write on.

How did he get a pen? He "plucked a hollow reed", and he

"made a rural pen".

What does that mean? He took a hollow stalk, such as an oat straw or a weed, and cut it in the form of a pen.

What is a "rural pen"? "Rural" means belonging to the country. The pen was not made as ours are. The shepherd wrote about sheep and other things belonging to country life.

How did he get any ink? He took "water" from the stream and "stained" it so that it would leave a mark something like our ink.

Yes, the paper, the pen, and the ink would not be so good as at present, but they would serve as a beginning.

REPRODUCTION

1. Where was the musician?
2. What kind of instrument was he playing?
3. Where was the child?
4. What was the child's second request?
5. What was his third request?
6. How was the shepherd able to write?
7. Why did the child wish him to write?

(The pupils may not understand "rural", "valley", "pipes", so the teacher should give such further explanation as the different cases demand.)

THE BABY SWALLOW

(First Reader, page 103)

The aim of this lesson is to teach, by means of a story, the moral of trusting in God and trying to do one's best.

The teacher should introduce the lesson by inquiring of the pupils if they have ever watched a young bird learning to fly. Its timidity and the anxiety of the mother-bird should be especially emphasized. A brief reference to the swallow might also be in place, though this is not essential, as the poet has selected it merely as a type of birds in general, and almost any other bird would answer his purpose as well. The rapidity and grace of the swallow's flight, and its habit of constructing its nest of mud under the eaves and in other sheltered places about buildings, are the main points to be noted.

What is the lesson about? About a baby swallow learning to fly.

What do the first four stanzas tell us? His fears.

And the last three? The success of his effort.

What do you see in the picture? A tower with a bell in it.

What name is given here for tower? Turret ("Turret" means a little tower.)

From its sound, what do you think "belfry" means? The place where the bell is.

What, then, is a "belfry turret"? A tower where a bell is hung.

On what part of the tower had the bird its nest? The front.

What word does the poet use to express that? "Breast".

What has been beating against the tower for years? The wind, sun, rain, snow.

What one word would stand for all these? Weather.

Explain "weather-beaten".

In perching on its nest, what does the baby swallow seem ready to do? To fly.

What other words might the Mother-Bird use instead of "courage"? "Don't be afraid."

How many wings are meant by "either wing"?

In this stanza, what is the "Mother-Bird" doing? Giving the little bird instructions in the way to begin flying.

Describe how he is to begin.

How does the baby feel about it? He feels afraid.

What word tells you this? "Pauses."

What does he think is deep? The distance between the tower and the ground.

Why is the bird afraid to attempt to fly? It is so far to the ground and his "wings" seem very "small".

Why is the "Mother" not afraid to let her baby try? She knows that God will carry him safely.

How does she know this? Because "He" had "carried" her.

When? When she was as small as the baby swallow is now.

Why does the "Mother" tell him this? To encourage him to make the attempt.

How does the baby swallow make his start? He "spreads out his wings" as far as he can and "springs" out.

Which stanza has almost the same form as this? The second.

What is he surprised to find? That he is able to fly.

How does he feel after that about flying? He is no longer afraid.

PREPARATION

What is he able to do well? To steer.

What does this mean? To fly in any direction he wishes.

How does the "Mother" feel over her baby's success? She feels glad.

To whom does she give thanks? To God.

How does she do so? By singing a song of thankfulness.

What can we learn from this story? That, if we really try to do a difficult thing, we can usually succeed; that sometimes a thing that looks hard is really very easy when we try to do it.

Tell this story in your own words. Tell any similar story you know.

THE BROOK

(First Reader, page 110)

PREPARATION

You stood on the bridge and looked at the stream. What did you see? I saw some little fishes. I saw my image. I saw some bright stones.

It is no wonder you looked at the stream when it shows you so many things. What were the fishes doing? They were swimming. They would dart after some crumbs that we dropped into the water.

Why were the fishes there? That is their home.

Yes, they like to live in the clear water. Mary says she saw her image. What have you at home that shows you your image? The mirror.

Yes, the brook is somewhat like the mirror. Did you see images of any other things? Yes, I saw images of the trees, and some stones, and I saw the images of the ducks that were swimming.

Willie says that he saw some pretty pebbles. Does the brook make any noise? Yes, it seems to sing when it runs over the pebbles, but in the deep places it does not make a noise.

PRESENTATION

Now I shall read you a little poem about a brook. (Read with emphasis, even with slight exaggeration.) Now, where did this brook begin? In "a fountain".

What is that? A spring of water.

Where was the fountain? "In a mountain".

What is that? A high hill.

Was it very large where it started? No, the lesson says it was only "Drops of water" and it trickled "through the grasses".

What does it mean by "Trickling through the grasses"? It means that there was so little of it that the blades of grass seemed almost to check its source.

Did it run very fast at first? No, the lesson says that it "started" "Slow".

Did it run any faster after that? Yes, "Soon it darted", and it was "Hurrying".

What caused it to dart and hurry? The ground was steeper, and it had to run more quickly.

Where was it running? Down "to the sea", where it would be lost in the other water.

Did it grow any larger before it came to the sea? Yes, it grew "Swift and strong", and it widened "very fast".

What caused it to widen? Other little brooks ran into it and made it wider.

Now, the brook is said to be like a person. Can you point out any words that make you think it was like a person? Yes, it hurries just as children hurry.

In the next stanza, the lesson says it was "Glad". Why was it glad? It was glad that the "Children" came to play on its banks.

Yes, it felt just as you feel when your friends come over to your house to play. Do you see any other words that make you think it is like a person? Yes, it is "Swift and strong and happy". It rushes and it sings.

What is it like now? It is like a big, strong, happy boy.

Why did the children come to play on its banks? They came to pick the flowers.

What line shows you that? "Blossoms floating." The children picked the flowers and threw some on the stream to watch the current carry them away.

What else were the children doing? They were sailing toy boats in the water.

What words show you that? "Mimic boating."

What else did the children enjoy? They liked to see the "Fishes darting past" them. The fishes were timid.

The brook makes some very pleasant sounds. What words show you that? "Rippling", "Bubbling", "singing", "ringing".

When does the water make these sounds? When it is running "over pebbles" or down the steep places.

You must fancy you hear the brook make its gentle music when it is running over the pebbles. What does the water look like when it ripples? It is not smooth; it has tiny waves upon it.

You have heard the water bubble and gurgle, and then, when the stream grows large and runs faster, you can hear it "singing" and "ringing" in the distance. The poet tells us some pretty things about the brook. Tell me some of them. It was "Cool and clear and free".

Why was it "Cool"? It had flowed among the grasses and had come from a spring in a mountain.

Why was it "clear"? It was such pure water that you could see the stones at the bottom of the brook.

Why does the poet say it was "free"? There were no logs nor big stones to stop its course. It ran freely on its way.

Do you see any other words that describe its appearance? It is "Flecked with shade and sun".

Now "Flecked" is a hard word. It means *spotted* or *striped*. Can you tell me what that means? Sometimes the brook is bright and shining and, in some places, it is shaded by the trees or by the clouds. You can see bright patches on the water.

Now you have told me many wonderful things about this brook; where it began and where it ended, how it grew, how it sang, how glad it was to see the children, and how the children played with it, and how it looked. What does it tell us at first? It tells us where it began.

In the next stanza? It runs a little faster.

In the next? It was glad to see the children.

In the next? The children were playing with it.

In the next? It ran bubbling and singing into the sea.

MEMORIZATION

Now we shall learn the words of this pretty lesson, taking the first stanza to-day. Let us take the first three lines. Now all the lines. Let each one be ready to repeat it. See whether you can say the first stanza to-morrow, and then we shall learn some more.

CHAPTER V
FORM II
ILLUSTRATIVE LESSONS

MY SHADOW

(Second Reader, page 3)

AIM

The aim of the lesson is to make the poem so lifelike that it will seem to each pupil as though the shadow and the words were his own.

PRESENTATION

After the poem has been read to give a general idea of the story, the teacher should proceed with it in detail, much in the same spirit as he would carry on a bright conversation with the pupils about something in which they were all equally interested.

Stanza I

How do I know my shadow is very fond of me? He "goes in and out with me".

What does that mean? It means he goes wherever I go.

What is "the use of him"? That "is more than I can see".

What is he like? He is just "like me from the heels up to the head".

What does he do when I go to bed? He jumps into bed "before me".

MEMORIZATION

Now, children, four of you may each recite one line. What have you, Susie? "I have a little shadow that goes in and out with me."

What is the use of your shadow, John? "And what can be the use of him is more than I can see."

What is he like, Mary? "He is very, very like me from the

heels up to the head."

When do you see him jump ahead of you? "And I see him jump before me, when I jump into my bed."

Note.—Each pupil's expression should reveal an active imagination and hearty response to the spirit of the selection. The whole should be very lifelike and real. Some pupil should be asked to recite or read the whole stanza.

Stanza II

What is there funny about the shadow? "The funniest thing about him is the way he likes to grow."

How is that? "He sometimes shoots up" very tall all at once, and then he dwindles down to nothing.

How would you expect him "to grow"? I would expect him "to grow" as I do.

How is that? Oh, that is "very slow".

The author says "like proper children". What does that mean? That means like real children.

What shows that he sometimes grows up very, very quickly? The poet says he "shoots up".

What other words tell the same thing? "Like an india-rubber ball."

How is that? The ball goes up quickly with a bounce, and the shadow seems to spring up in the same way.

READING AND MEMORIZATION

Let two or three children read the stanza. In the first line, the voice should show how funny it all is; in the second, the demureness of the "proper" child and the slowness of the growth should be revealed in the reading; in the third and fourth lines, there should be an imitative response to the sudden up-growth of the shadow and to the childish surprise at his dwindling into nothing.

Memorization should be conducted as shown in Stanza I, above. There should be no evidence of task or effort in the recitation; it is very necessary that it be spontaneous and full of enjoyment for the pupils.

Stanza III

The shadow knows very little about one thing. What is that? He has no "notion of how children ought to play".

How does he "make a fool of me"? "In every sort of way."

Well, give one way. He mimics me.

Where does he stay? He stays right "close beside me".

Why does he do that? He does that because "he's a coward".

How would you feel about doing the same thing? I would feel ashamed of myself.

Reading and recitation of this stanza should now be conducted as indicated in Stanzas I and II, above.

Stanza IV

Did you ever manage to get away from your shadow? Yes, I did.

Tell us about how you did it. Well, "One morning, very early", I got up "before the sun" did, and went out in the flower garden. I looked around for my shadow, and I found he "had stayed at home behind me" in bed.

What is he called for doing that? He is called "an arrant sleepy-head".

Give another word in place of "arrant" that will mean the same thing. He was a thorough and shameless "sleepy-head".

What was the real cause of his staying behind? There was "none of him at all", because the sun was not up.

What will happen when the sun does come up? Then my shadow will suddenly show himself again.

Now, if you would like to have another stanza, telling about what happened when the sun came up, just try your best to write one.

Here is another that was written once at the end of the lesson:

But when the dear old sun came up above the trees,
My frisky little shadow came out into the breeze;
I didn't see him coming, but, when I turned around,
His head was at the window, and he lay along the ground.

ONE, TWO, THREE

(Second Reader, page 21)

AIM

To enable the pupils to understand the beauty and pathos of the selection.

To arouse in them a sympathy for those who are weak.

PREPARATION

How many of you like to play games? Everybody.

Name some of the games you play. Ball, tag, hide-and-seek,

etc.

With whom do you like to play? With boys and girls of our own age.

PRESENTATION

Here is a story that tells about two people playing a game. (The selection is read aloud by the teacher.)

What is the story about? An "old lady" and a little boy playing "Hide-and-Go-Seek".

What relation were they? The old lady was the boy's "Grandma".

Let us look at the story again, and see if they enjoyed their game as much as you do yours. Is there anything in the first stanza that tells us they were having a good time? "The way that they played together was beautiful to see."

What was beautiful about it? They were so kind to each other. It was pleasant to see an old lady and a little boy having such a happy time playing together, and understanding each other so well.

How do you feel, as you read the second stanza? I feel sorry for the boy because he is lame.

Any other reason for feeling sorry for him? He is "thin", as though he had been sick a long time.

In what way are he and his Grandma alike? Neither of them can run or jump.

Do you feel more sorry for the Grandma or for the little boy? I feel more sorry for the boy, because he may never be able to run around, and his Grandma could when she was young.

Describe the picture you see in the third stanza. I see an old lady and a little boy sitting "under the maple tree". The little boy has a pair of crutches beside him. The "sunlight" is shining through the leaves, and it is a warm summer's day, or they would not be sitting out. There is a house near them.

What game were they playing? "Hide-and-Go-Seek."

Would you know it from looking at them? No, because they are sitting still, and when we play the game, we run around and hide.

How did they play it? They thought in turn of some place to hide and imagined they were hiding in it; they had three guesses to find out the place.

Whose turn was it to hide? The old lady's, because the boy is guessing where she is.

Where did he find her at last? In "Papa's big bed-room", in "the clothes-press".

Is there anything else spoken about that was in the bed-room? There was a "little cupboard".

Why does he mention the cupboard? He often thinks of it. He likes it.

Why? His mother's "things used to be" in it.

Why does he say "used to be"? That tells us that they are not there any longer.

Why? I think his mother is dead.

Who takes care of him now? His grandmother lives with him and looks after him.

Why does the boy say "It can't be the little cupboard"? They both think too much of it to want to use it in connection with their play.

How did the boy enjoy the game? Very much, because it says he laughed "with glee".

How did the Grandma enjoy it? She was glad to see the boy happy.

Do old ladies usually like to play games? No, they generally prefer to read or sew.

Why was she playing with the boy? She loved him and was sorry he was lame.

Could he do anything for his Grandma? He could talk to her, and keep her from being lonely. When he grows older, he can read to her.

Describe the picture you see in the ninth stanza. I see the old lady, with her hands covering her face, while she guesses where the boy is hidden.

In the last stanza, why does the author use so many "olds", in speaking of the Grandmother? He wants to make us feel she is quite old.

Why does he say "dear" so often? He wants to show how very kind she was to the lame boy.

Why does he say the boy was "half-past three", instead of three and a half years old? It sounds better the way he says it. It suggests the clock's time.

Give me some other titles for this poem. "The Chums", "A Queer Game", "The Two Playmates".

DANDELIONS

(Second Reader, page 30)

AIM

To lead the pupils to perceive and appreciate how the poet uses personification and comparison.

PRESENTATION

This poem should be studied in the spring, when the dandelions are in bloom. A nature study lesson should precede the literature lesson. The pupils should be required to observe when the dandelions begin to make their appearance; at what time of the day they are most conspicuous; after what kind of night they are to be found in greatest profusion; what change occurs in the structure of the flowers as they grow older; how long a time usually elapses between the first appearance of the flowers and this change; what the white, downy part of the flower constitutes; what eventually becomes of this part.

Introduce the lesson by a brief conversation about military operations. Describe how one army tries to seize a strategic position, sometimes a hill, where the men can fix their guns and command the surrounding country. If this lesson could be presented without the pupils knowing the title (by writing the poem on the black-board, for instance), there would be the added interest of solving a riddle, namely, what the poet is describing.

What is a real "trooper band"? A band of soldiers on horseback.

And what are real "veterans"? Old soldiers who have seen much service in war.

What is actually meant by the "trooper band"? The dandelions when they first come out.

What is the phrase that suggests that they are dandelions? "Yellow coats."

What does the author actually mean by the "veterans"? The dandelions, when they have gone to seed.

What phrase suggests this? "Their trembling heads and gray."

Where did the "trooper band" make their appearance? On the hillside.

When? On a "showery night and still".

Why is such a night selected? Because it makes the dandelions bloom in great numbers.

To what is the coming of the dandelions compared? To an army taking possession of a hill.

What words tell how they came? "Without a sound of warning", "surprised", "We were not waked by bugle notes", "No cheer our dreams invaded".

Explain "surprised the hill". Marched upon it when they were least expected, and seized it.

Give the meaning of "held it in the morning". Had undisputed possession of it.

Tell, in your own words, how the dandelions came. Suddenly and unexpectedly.

How did this attack differ from a real military attack? There were no notes of the bugle or shouts of the soldiers to announce the capture of the hill.

Change "No cheer our dreams invaded" into prose order, and explain the meaning. No cheer invaded our dreams. Our sleep was not disturbed by the victorious shouts of soldiers.

How did the coats of the soldiers you have seen differ in colour from those of the dandelions?

What is the meaning of "at dawn"? The first appearance of light in the morning.

"Green slopes"? Grassy hillsides.

"Paraded"? Marched up and down.

About what time has elapsed between the incident of the first stanza and that of the second? Probably a week or thereabouts.

What deed is referred to in the first stanza? The seizure of the hill.

What is meant by "idly walking"? Without any definite purpose in view.

"Marked"? Noticed.

About what were the veterans probably "talking"? About their military exploits in years gone by.

What words are suitably used in describing these veterans? "Trembling" and "gray" suggest old age.

Arrange "their trembling heads and gray" in ordinary prose order. Their gray and trembling heads.

Why should the veterans be filled with "pride"? Because of the brave deeds they had done.

Why did they laugh? Perhaps, because of some amusing occurrences they had seen.

What characteristics of the dandelions suggest these fancies regarding the veterans? The heads of the dandelions are white. As they sway in the breeze on their slender stalks, they incline their heads toward one another in much the same way as people do in conversation.

Why is the "laughter" said to be "noiseless"? Because human beings could not be expected to hear the laughter of the dandelions.

What expression would you be likely to use, instead of "welladay"? Alas!

What is meant by "they blew away"? The seeds of the flowers were scattered far and wide.

What do you like about this poem? (1) Its charming poetic fancies. (2) The fitness of the comparisons.

Point out clearly how the appearance of the dandelions resembled a military attack, and how, in the later stage of their life history, they resembled veteran soldiers.

THE BLIND MEN AND THE ELEPHANT

(Second Reader, page 56)

AIM

The aim of the lesson should be, not only to lead the pupils to enjoy the humour of the poem, but also to appreciate the lesson it teaches. It affords a fine opportunity for the development of conversational powers in the pupils.

The pupils should be encouraged to talk freely, and the questions should often call for quite lengthy answers.

PREPARATION

Who has seen an elephant? You have, Henry? Well, tell us something about him. He was very large. One of our barn doors is twelve feet high and six feet wide, and father said the elephant would just be able to go through that door. If he was in the schoolroom, his back would reach almost to the ceiling. His ears were bigger than the top of my desk. His trunk was twice as long as father's cane, and was nearly as big around at the upper end as a bag of wheat, and the lower end was as small as my leg is below the knee. His tusks were hard and white, one on each side of his trunk, and were longer than father's arm. His tail was small. It did not seem to be as long as one of his tusks. His legs were larger around than the trunk of the biggest apple tree in our orchard. His skin was something like a hog's skin, only thicker, and he had no hair. His whole body was a dirty, dark colour.

That is a fairly good description, Henry. You have helped us to picture a very large elephant.

PRESENTATION

As you have read this poem to yourselves, tell me what it is about. It is about six blind men "Who went to see the elephant".

As they were blind, how could they see him? They couldn't see him as we do, but they could feel him, and that was to them what seeing is to us.

In what way was feeling the same to them as seeing is to us? It was their way of knowing the animal, and that is just what seeing is to us.

Where did this happen? It happened in Indostan.

I told you to look for Indostan in Asia. Point it out on the map. (A pupil points to it.)

What are we told about these men? They gave much of their time to study.

What do you suppose was their favourite way of finding out things? This lesson makes me think that they liked to find out things by their own efforts.

Why do you think that? Because it says that they wanted to "satisfy" their minds by their own "observations".

In what other ways do boys and girls satisfy their minds about new things? By asking questions about them until the answers satisfy them.

What other way do you use sometimes? We read books to learn about many new things.

What did the first man learn? He thought he had learned that the elephant was "like a wall".

Why do you say thought? He hadn't really learned it. He stopped making observations just as soon as he had one idea.

Why do you think he did that? I think he was in a hurry to be the first to state what he knew.

What words in the poem suggest that idea to you? The words "At once began to bawl".

How did this man come to think the elephant was "like a wall"? He fell against the animal's huge side, and it made him think of a wall.

What was the second man's opinion about the elephant? He thought the animal was "like a spear".

Account for that idea. He felt one of the elephant's tusks, and formed his opinion without going any further.

And what about the third man? The third man put his hands on the elephant's trunk and felt it all over, but as he did not go any further, he declared that the elephant was "like a snake", because it was the only thing, as far as he knew, that squirmed about as the trunk did.

What did the fourth man do? The fourth man felt the big front legs and declared the elephant was "like a tree".

Tell us about the fifth man. The fifth man happened to touch the ear. He felt all over it but nowhere else, so he said the elephant was "like a fan".

And what had the sixth man to say? The sixth man had caught hold of the elephant's tail, and when he had felt all over it, he declared the elephant was "like a rope".

What conclusion did they come to in the end? They didn't come to any conclusion. They argued and argued for a long time, and each man was stubborn and stuck to "his own opinion".

GENERALIZATION

In what respects were they all alike?

1. Each one felt just one part of the animal and took the part for the whole.
2. Each was in a hurry to give his opinion and did not take time to form a good one.
3. Each man was stubborn and probably refused to feel where the others had felt.

If they could be in your place, how would they see themselves? They would see how foolish they had been, and each would see that the others were as nearly right as he himself was.

What lesson for ourselves can we learn from this? It teaches us not to be in a hurry in giving our opinions.

What do we learn from the dispute mentioned in the last verse? We learn from it that, when our own opinions about anything are firmly fixed, it does no good to argue about the matter.

In what way could they have arrived at the same conclusions? If each had done all that each of the others did, they would have agreed about the elephant.

In what way were these men really blind? They could not, or would not, see the viewpoint of others. There may be a mental blindness, as well as a physical blindness.

Here are two lines that you may memorize, as they fit the

lesson very well:

> Convince a man against his will,
> He's of the same opinion still.

THE LORD IS MY SHEPHERD

(Second Reader, page 203)

AIM

To lead the pupils to appreciate the beauty and power of the language of this Biblical lesson, and to feel a confidence in God's protection and support.

PRESENTATION

The teacher should talk with the pupils about the great flocks of sheep in Eastern lands. They require a shepherd to lead them to pastures where the grass is long and sweet, and to protect them from the wild animals.

This Psalm is called the "Shepherd Psalm" because it was written by David, after he became a king. He remembered the time when he was a shepherd boy and used to spend his days and nights in the fields with the sheep, and how he once killed a lion and a bear that came to attack his flock; and he thought to himself that God had cared for him all his life just as he himself used to care for his little lambs, so at last he put his thoughts into the words of this Twenty-third Psalm.

There are two metaphors in this Psalm. In the first is developed, through the figure of a shepherd and his flock, God's care of His people.

> What are the feelings of the sheep toward the shepherd? They feel confident that he will supply them with food; he will lead them to the "green pastures" and to the "still waters" by the wells and fountains, where they will neither hunger nor thirst.
>
> What does the expression "lie down" infer? A sense of rest and security. The sheep can lie down in the "green pastures" and feel confident that the shepherd is able and willing to protect them from danger.
>
> In what way do we resemble the sheep? We are dependent upon the Lord for our supply of spiritual and material needs, and for guidance and protection along the path of everyday life.
>
> What does the Psalmist mean when he says: "He restoreth my soul"? "Soul" means, in Hebrew, the "life," or "one's self". The Lord restores and brings back His people, when wandering into forbidden places.
>
> Explain the next line. As the shepherd goes before and leads his sheep by the right paths, avoiding all dangers, so the Lord leads His people into "the paths of righteousness".

What does "for His name's sake" mean? He has undertaken to guide His people safely and will do it for the honour of His name.

In the next section, whom is the Psalmist addressing? He is speaking to the Lord.

What words show that he is still using the figure of the shepherd and the sheep? "Through the valley"; "Thy rod and thy staff".

What does the first line mean? Some paths that are right paths for us to walk in still lead through perilous places; and this is the way the Psalmist refers to this fact in shepherd life.

How should we feel? The Lord accompanies us, and we should "fear no evil". The sheep follow the shepherd with absolute confidence, and our attitude toward "the Good Shepherd" should be the same.

What words show that danger is sometimes close? Death sometimes comes so close that it almost seems to cast a shadow.

What does the "rod" represent? The rod is the sign of authority, and represents the defence and protection afforded by the shepherd to the sheep, when in danger from robbers or wild beasts.

What does the "staff" represent? The staff denotes support and guidance, and is used for aiding the sheep in places of need, even along peaceful ways. The expression "Thy rod and thy staff" covers the whole round of protecting care.

Here the figure is changed. In the second metaphor God is represented as a host with the Psalmist as a guest at a banquet.

"Thou preparest a table before me." The Lord makes provision for man's needs. He does so openly, publicly ("in the presence of mine enemies").

In what other way does the Lord show His care for His people? The Psalmist says: "Thou hast anointed my head with oil."

To what does this refer? In the East, it was the custom to pour an ointment of great fragrance on the heads of the guests of honour at a feast.

How does the Psalmist further picture the goodness of God? He fills our "cup" till it is overflowing.

What is the thought in the last two lines? The confidence of the Psalmist in the Lord, that as He has led and guided him in the past, so His "goodness and mercy" "shall follow" him "all the days of his life," and he will live forever in intimate communion with Him.

What do you like about the selection? The spirit of gratitude and confidence in those who enjoy God's benefits. The nature of some of these benefits is made plain to us by the pictures of the "green pastures", the "still waters", "the rod and staff", and the prepared "table".

CHAPTER VI
FORM III
ILLUSTRATIVE LESSONS

HIDE AND SEEK

(Third Reader, page 50)

AIM

To lead the pupils to appreciate the exquisite music of the language and the pathos of the story.

PRESENTATION

What does the poem describe? It describes a father's love for his son.

There are two distinct parts. What does each part describe? The first two stanzas describe a game of "Hide and Seek" between the father and the boy, and the last two, the father's intense longing for the boy whom he has lost.

What kind of day is described in the first stanza? A bright and calm June day.

What things suggest this? Sleeping trees, still winds, wandering clouds, "noonday silence".

What does the writer represent the trees and the winds to be? Persons—the trees having the ability to sleep, and the winds to move or keep still. This is called personification.

What are "fleecy clouds"? Clouds that are white and downy.

The poet speaks of them as "flocks". What is the comparison intended? The comparison of the clouds to flocks of white sheep that, instead of wandering across a meadow, are wandering across the sky.

What does the word "wandered" suggest? That the clouds are moving along slowly and leisurely without any purpose in view. They are doing this because the "winds are still".

What is meant by saying that they "Have wandered past the

hill"? They have gone below the horizon at the hilltop and cannot be seen. The sky is thus clear of clouds.

What causes "the noonday silence"? The heat of the mid-day has silenced even the songs of the birds. Compare Keats:

> When all the birds are faint with the hot sun
> And hide in cooling trees.

How is the silence broken? By the voice of the little boy hunting for his father.

What do the words of the tune he is singing constitute? The rules of the game. The one hiding must respond "Coo-ee" each time the one searching calls.

Where is his father? In a "leafy nook" in the woods.

What does the question "Shall I let him pass?" seem to indicate? That his father hesitates for a moment to reveal himself.

What does he do, however? He gives the boy the signal—a "low, soft whistle". He cannot "let him pass".

What is shown in the last long line of the stanza? That the man enters into the spirit of the game with the same zest as the boy.

What feeling exists between the two? A feeling of perfect good-fellowship and affection.

Explain, "you're it". Your turn to hunt, mine to hide.

What further rules of the game are given here? (Every boy and girl will know these.)

What change in feeling is there between the first two stanzas and the last two? A sudden transition from gaiety and light-heartedness to sorrow.

What has happened? The boy is dead.

Why is "Long ago" repeated? It emphasizes the idea and adds to the pathos of the line. The time has seemed long because of the intensity of the father's grief. Happiness makes time pass quickly, not so grief.

How does the poet suggest the idea that the game is still being continued though it is now an inexpressibly sad one? He speaks of the boy as having left his father as if to hide, of his father as seeking him "high and low", of his being safely "hidden" "in some pleasant place", of the father as being unable to hear his "Coo-ee".

What is really meant by seeking him "high and low"? The thought of his boy is ever with him. He unconsciously looks for his face wherever he goes.

What is the "pleasant place"? Paradise.

How could you describe the short lines, "Far away", etc., down to the end of the stanza? As the call of a broken heart to the boy.

Where is the idea contained in "Far away" expressed before? In "Hidden safe and happy in some pleasant place".

And where is the thought, "Many a day", repeated? "Long ago he left me, long and long ago."

How is the father continually reminded of his boy? By the "Birds" and "Flowers"—everything that he loved is charged with memories of him.

What light is thrown upon the little fellow's interests? He loved the out-of-doors, the things of nature.

What ray of sunshine breaks through the clouds of the father's grief? The conviction that his boy "is waiting" for him till he comes.

What is the meaning of the line, "Love may hide itself", etc.? The little boy's love may for the moment be hidden, but it is everlasting. The father's love is likewise everlasting. This is sufficient ground for believing that they will some day be united.

The reading of this poem by the pupils will show whether they feel its joy, its sadness, and its hope.

AN APPLE ORCHARD IN THE SPRING

(Third Reader, page 60)

AIM

To lead the pupils to appreciate the beauty of an apple orchard in the spring and the music of the language used in describing it.

PREPARATION

This lesson should be taken when the apple orchards are in bloom. The teacher should prepare the pupils for it, by asking them to observe the blossoms, their colours and odours, the songs of the birds, and the sounds of the streams.

PRESENTATION

Read the poem describing these. What is the main theme of the lesson? The poet tells us how much we have missed if we have not "seen an apple orchard in the spring".

What is his theme in the first three stanzas? The beauty of an apple orchard.

What, in the last stanza? His memory of it.

In what order does he describe the blossoms? In the first stanza, the buds are turning white; in the second, they are unfolding; and in the third, the petals are dropping.

Where does the author suppose the reader to be standing, in the first stanza? Outside the orchard, where it is possible to see "the spreading trees" and all the orchard at once.

Where, in the next two stanzas, is he supposed to be? He is plucking the blossoms and walking under the trees.

What senses are appealed to in the first stanza? Sight—"seen an apple orchard". Hearing—"mavis sings its story".

What senses are appealed to in the second stanza? Touch—"plucked the apple blossoms", "touch them a delight". Smell—"caught their subtle odours". Sight—"Pink buds pouting at the light", "Crumpled petals baby white".

What senses are appealed to in the third? Sight—"pink cascades". Hearing—"silver brooklets brawling", "cuckoo bird soft calling".

Show the appropriateness of "hoary", "wealth of promised glory", "pouting", "pink cascades", "silver brooklets brawling", "wonder of the spring", "precious", "tender".

What Canadian birds could be substituted for the mavis and the cuckoo? The robins, warblers, and goldfinches.

Lead the pupils to examine the arrangement of the rhythm and the refrain, so that they will appreciate the music of the verse. Let each pupil show his appreciation by reading the stanza he likes best.

LITTLE DAFFYDOWNDILLY

(Third Reader, page 223)

The teacher should require the pupils to read the lesson through and then to reproduce its main incidents without any regard to their allegorical significance. Such headings as the following might be suggested by the pupils, and these would serve to guide in this reproduction:

1. Daffydowndilly's dislike of the schoolmaster
2. His decision to run away from school
3. His meeting with the stranger who accompanies him on his journey
4. The haymakers
5. The carpenters
6. The soldiers
7. The merry-makers

8. His discovery of his companion's identity
9. The lesson that he learned.

Having thus obtained the literal meaning of the story—a matter of little difficulty—it remains to get its deeper significance. It is hardly probable that many pupils will be disposed to regard the story as literally true, yet few will be likely, upon a first reading, to see the principle that underlies it. In order to arrive at this, the teacher may proceed as follows:

> Are there any parts of the story that strike you as improbable? (1) The reference to Mr. Toil's long residence upon the earth. (2) The frequent meetings with Mr. Toil's brothers. (3) Daffydowndilly's slowness in discovering another brother in the person of his companion. (4) Their travelling all day in a circle.
>
> If the story is literally untrue or improbable, what object might Hawthorne have had in view in writing it? Perhaps he wished to teach some lesson; perhaps there is a meaning hidden beneath the story.
>
> Let us discover what that hidden meaning is? What does the name "Toil" suggest to you? Work.
>
> What, then, may Mr. Toil represent? Work.
>
> And what may his brothers represent? Different kinds of work.
>
> With this idea in mind, we shall now try to understand what each adventure really means. How are we prepared for Daffydowndilly's troubles with the schoolmaster and for his later unpleasant experience? The author tells us that he "took no delight in labour of any kind".
>
> What flower did he resemble? The daffodil. The boy's name is another form of the name of the flower.
>
> In what respect is he said to resemble a flower? He "loved to do only what was beautiful and agreeable, and took no delight in labour of any kind".
>
> Why is Mr. Toil first represented as a schoolmaster? Because it is at school that a boy is first introduced to real work. (This might be given a still more extended meaning. The school represents the preparation for our future vocation, whether it be in the schoolroom, or in an apprenticeship, or elsewhere. This involves hard work, and hence is, to some extent, at least, unpleasant.)
>
> What is meant by saying that Mr. Toil "had done more good ... than anybody else in the world"? Work does everybody good: (1) It keeps us out of mischief. Criminals often become so because of the lack of profitable employment. (2) It improves character. The people of the best and strongest character are those who have

had to work hard. (3) It makes the world happier. The most miserable people are those who have nothing to do.

"A very worthy character." Is "character" used in its usual sense here? It usually means what a person really *is*.

(Distinguish "character" and "reputation".)

Explain what is meant by saying that "he had dwelt upon earth ever since Adam was driven from the garden of Eden". Ever since that time man has had to work. God said to Adam (Genesis iii, 19), "In the sweat of thy face shalt thou eat bread".

Why is Mr. Toil represented as being such a disagreeable person? Because, to some people, work has many unpleasant features.

Any activity that has no compulsory elements in it is no longer work, but play. What is the real meaning of the paragraph describing the schoolmaster's method of discipline? The work of the school-room, being compulsory, and therefore disagreeable to idle boys, becomes exceedingly painful when long continued.

Contrast Daffydowndilly's previous life with his experience at school. Brought up under the indulgence of his mother, his life had been very pleasant. Now, introduced to real work, he finds life very unpleasant.

What gives us a suggestion as to the identity of the stranger whom Daffydowndilly met on the road? We are told that he was "trudging" "along the road", and that his voice "seemed hard and severe".

Why is "trudging" a better word than "walking"? It suggests effort, and hence work.

How does the form of the question, "Whence do you come so early, and whither are you going?" harmonize with the description of the stranger?

We are told that he had a "grave and sedate appearance", and the somewhat stilted form of the question is quite in harmony with this description.

Why had his voice "a sort of kindness in it"? Because moderate work, such as this walking early in the day, is not altogether unpleasant.

Explain "ingenuous disposition". How does Daffydowndilly show this?

What made his discovery of Mr. Toil among the labourers in the hayfield so unexpected? The circumstances and surroundings—"the sunshine", "the blue sky", the singing birds, the fragrant hay—were so pleasant that it was hard to see how anything so unpleasant as work could intrude there.

Why is Mr. Toil recognized in the owner of the field rather than among the labourers? In directing the activities of the men, as well as working himself, he is performing the most arduous labour of all.

Why does the stranger say the farmer is a "more disagreeable man" than his brother, the schoolmaster? Because the activities of farm life are more laborious than those of the school-room.

What expression that takes the form of a proverb is used in describing this incident? "To make hay while the sun shone."

Distinguish its meaning, as the author uses it, from its meaning as a proverb. The author uses it in its literal meaning. The farmer must make the most of fine weather and sunshine in curing ("making") his hay, for, if rain comes after it is cut, it will be more or less injured. Used as a proverb, the expression means that one should seize the opportunities presented and make the most of them.

What does Hawthorne mean by placing a Mr. Toil at the head of the company of soldiers? Military movements, though very attractive to the eye, really involve work. Soldiers find their activities very toilsome, especially after the novelty has worn off.

Why is Mr. Toil placed even among the dancers? The pursuit of pleasure soon becomes wearisome, and hence toilsome.

Why is the fiddler represented as a Frenchman? France, as a whole, is reputed to be the gayest and sprightliest of nations.

What is meant by saying that "those who have known him best think him still more disagreeable than his brothers"? Those who devote themselves entirely to the pursuit of pleasure find it more toilsome and disagreeable than ordinary work. People frequently say, after a day given up to pleasure, that they are more tired than if they had worked hard all day.

In which of the incidents of the story does it seem least likely that Mr. Toil would be met with? In the incident of the merry-makers.

In which, most likely? The incident of the haymakers.

How has Hawthorne apparently arranged Daffydowndilly's experiences? He has so arranged them that in each successive incident we are more surprised at meeting with Mr. Toil. Each one seems to promise less probability of his presence than the preceding.

Why had Daffydowndilly not recognized his companion before? His voice had been kind and his manner agreeable in the early stages of the journey.

Interpret this as has been done in the case of the other incidents. The early part of Daffydowndilly's journey had been pleasant, owing to the freedom from school and the interesting experiences by the way. But, as the day drew on, he gradually grew tired, and then it was that he recognized that walking is work.

What lesson did he learn? That he could not get away from work. It is to be found everywhere, in the most unexpected places, and one cannot escape from it by changing his occupation.

What is meant by Daffydowndilly's finding Mr. Toil's ways more agreeable upon better acquaintance? When he grew accustomed to his work, he found that it was not so very unpleasant after all; "that diligence is not a whit more toilsome than sport or idleness".

What is Mr. Toil's "smile of approbation"? The consciousness of work well done.

Tell the pupils that this story is an Allegory. They have probably read other stories of a similar nature, and may be asked to frame a simple definition. An Allegory is a story, not literally true, containing incidents that have a deeper meaning than is apparent on the surface. Its purpose is to teach some moral truth or universal principle. It differs from the Parable in being longer and more complex.

When the pupils reproduce the story, it will be well to adhere to the allegorical form, and not attempt to give its significance.

MOONLIGHT SONATA

(Third Reader, page 285)

AIM

To lead the pupils to appreciate the importance of details in the construction of a story.

PREPARATION

The teacher will have told the pupils a few facts about Beethoven and, if possible, will have shown them his picture. He will also have asked them to read the lesson at home and become familiar with the story.

PRESENTATION

What is the main point in the story? The circumstances under which the musician wrote the "Moonlight Sonata".

What is a sonata? It is a musical composition which consists of movements fast or slow, sad or playful, according to the varying mood of the composer.

Where was the scene? In Bonn in Prussia.

When? On a moonlight winter's evening.

Who were the two persons? Beethoven and the writer.

Notice that these three important facts are all told briefly at the beginning.

Why had the writer called on the musician? He wished to take him for a walk and afterwards take him home with him to supper.

Had he any reason except the desire for Beethoven's company? Yes, Beethoven's health was not good, his hearing was becoming impaired, and the writer evidently thought he needed rest and recreation. These circumstances led to an important result.

What happened next? In passing through a narrow street, Beethoven heard some one playing his "Sonata in F".

What were his feelings? Surprise to hear it in such a place and delight at the excellence of the playing.

How did he show his feelings? By exclamations, questions, and short sentences.

What is told in the next three paragraphs? They describe a conversation.

Who are speaking? A brother and sister.

What are they saying? The sister is lamenting that she cannot "go to the concert at Cologne" and her brother reminds her of their poverty. Then she wishes that "for once in her life" she "could hear some really good music".

What happens next? Beethoven decides to enter the house.

How does the writer impress this fact on the reader? By giving the argument between himself and Beethoven.

What were the latter's reasons? The player had "feeling, genius, understanding", and these qualities are so rarely found that Beethoven could not neglect them.

Explain these terms. The player showed refined feeling in her interpretation of the music, genius in her skill on the piano, and thorough understanding of the composer's purposes in the composition.

Was it only for his own pleasure that the composer entered? No, he wished to give pleasure to one who could so well appreciate his work.

Describe the scene. A young shoemaker is seated at his work. He is pale from the effects of confinement and toil. A young girl with an abundance of light hair is leaning on an "old-fashioned piano".

What does this piano show? That their parents had very probably been lovers of music, and the piano may have been an heirloom.

What comes next? The musician explains the reasons for his intrusion.

How did the brother look upon it? The young man seemed annoyed at first.

How was this annoyance overcome? The manner of Beethoven was so comical and pleasant that the young man's annoyance passed away.

How had Beethoven addressed the brother and sister? His manner was very confused. He wished to conceal his name, and yet wished to give pleasure to the young girl.

How does he show his confusion? The sentences "I, I also ... play for you", are such halting ones. He does not make his sentences complete.

What was the next part of the conversation? The young man tells Beethoven that the "piano is so wretched" and they "have no music".

What is the purpose of this statement in the story? It shows Beethoven that the young girl is blind and plays these difficult compositions by ear.

How had she learned to play this Sonata? She had heard a lady "practising" it, and "walked to and fro" in front of the house in order "to listen to it".

What does this show? What a love of music and wonderful natural ability the young girl possessed.

What is the next action in the story? Beethoven plays.

Why did he play better than he had often done before large audiences? He realized how greatly his work was appreciated; and he was deeply touched by the thought of the young girl's blindness, her poverty, her skill, and her passion for good music.

What trifling occurrence now affects the story? The last candle in the house burned out, so the writer opened the shutters and admitted "a flood of brilliant moonlight".

What effect had this upon the composer? It changed the current of his thoughts and feelings.

How did he appear? "His head dropped upon his breast", and "his hands rested upon his knees".

What is the next action? The young shoemaker asks Beethoven who he is.

What did the composer answer? "He played the opening bars of the Sonata in F." This revealed his name. The writer says that the young people "covered his hands with tears and kisses".

What were their feelings? Their actions were expressions of their affection and admiration.

What takes place next? The brother and sister beseech him to play "once more".

What description is given here? Beethoven's appearance in the moonlight.

Describe him. He was very "massive" in size, his head was large and his features strong, and the light from the moon encircled his head. (Produce a picture, if possible, of Beethoven.)

Did he agree to play again? Yes, he said he would "improvise a Sonata to the Moonlight".

What does "improvise" mean? He would compose the music as he played.

Had this any relation to what goes before? Yes, the writer has told us how thoughtful he had been when the moonlight first streamed into the room. Now he is going to express his thoughts and feelings through the tones of the piano.

We said at the beginning that a Sonata was a musical composition consisting of various movements. What are the movements? In this case there is first, "a sad and infinitely lovely movement", then, "a wild, elfin passage in triple time", and lastly, "a breathless, hurrying, trembling" close.

Let us examine this description of the "Moonlight Sonata" more closely. What did the moonlight suggest to Beethoven? "Spirits" dancing in the moonlight.

What does the first movement suggest? The "moonlight" flowing "over the dark earth".

What does the second movement suggest? The wild dance of the "spirits on the lawn".

What does the last suggest? "Flight", "uncertainty", "impulsive terror".

What was the effect upon the listeners? They were left in a state of "wonder" and "emotion".

What musical terms are used to describe this music? *Interlude, triple time, agitato finale.*

Explain them. *Interlude* is a piece of music played between the main parts. *Triple time* is time, or rhythm, of three beats, or of three times three beats in a bar.

Give an example of triple time. It denotes sprightliness, as in the waltz. The *agitato finale* means the close of the passage with a hurrying movement.

What takes place next? Beethoven rose quickly, promised to come again, and hurried away.

Why did he hurry? He wished to write out the "Sonata" while it was still fresh in his mind.

What does the last short paragraph state? It tells that this was the origin of the "Moonlight Sonata".

Where is the theme of the whole lesson found? In the last sentence.

What has the writer told us? He has given us all the circumstances which combined to inspire Beethoven to compose this great work.

RECAPITULATION

Now let us review the story and collect these details. What are they? The time, place, the persons going for a walk, the narrow street, the wonderful playing, the conversation, the appearance of the young people, the blindness of the girl, her eagerness to hear "good music", the moonlight admitted, the recognition of Beethoven.

Yes, all these things had a combined effect upon the musician. If he had gone straight to supper, there would probably not have been a "Moonlight Sonata". This lesson illustrates how time, place, persons, and action are arranged to produce a well-told story.

LEAD, KINDLY LIGHT

(Third Reader, page 315)

AIM

To aid in the culture of a sensitive response to the spirit and language of the prayer.

PREPARATION

The teacher should talk with the pupils about a journey through the darkness, over dangerous bogs, swollen streams, and beside precipices.

PRESENTATION

Read the poem. In what form is this lesson? A prayer.

What is the prayer? The traveller asks for the guidance of the Holy Spirit. See notes on this lesson in the Manual on *The Ontario Readers*, pp. 166-7.

Describe his journey. "The night is dark", he is "far from home", he trusts to the light shining through the darkness to keep his feet from stumbling; he does not trouble himself about what lies far before him, he attends only to his footsteps one by one. He feels he can pass safely over the "moor", the "fen", the "crag", and the "torrent", by trusting to the guidance of the light. With the dawning of the day will come the reunion with his loved ones from whom he has been separated.

Explain the symbolism employed here. The poet speaks of himself as going through life like a traveller on a long journey, wherein he is constantly met by trials and temptations and cannot always know what is the right course to take. He acknowledges that he needs some stronger power than his own to direct his life and asks for the guidance of the Holy Spirit, content to trust himself to His leading in any dangers and difficulties that may arise in this life, and secure in the knowledge that "with the morn" he shall see once more those whom he has "loved" and "lost awhile".

What is the main thought of the first stanza? The traveller prays for guidance.

Of the second stanza? He states that he has not always been willing to ask for guidance, but had relied on his own reason.

Of the third stanza? He expresses his belief in the power and willingness of God to guide him aright.

What is the relation of the second stanza to the first one? It contrasts the poet's earlier attitude of mind toward God with that of later years, thus emphasizing the change that has taken place in his life.

Is the poet stronger in the second case than in the first? No; in the first, his ideal is higher and his humility greater, as he relies absolutely on the guidance of the Holy Spirit. In the second, relying only on his own reasoning powers to guide him, he made many humiliating failures.

Image the "moor", the "fen", the "crag", the "torrent", and "with the morn".

RECAPITULATION

Summarize the main thoughts and lead the pupils to bring out clearly the comparison between the traveller and the poet.

Give a brief account of the author's life.

LEAD, KINDLY LIGHT

(Third Reader, page 315)

AIM

To aid in the culture of a sensitive response to the spirit and language of the prayer.

TREATMENT

The teacher should read the poem aloud, to awaken respect for the deep humility, complete open-mindedness, and growing faith of the poet.

What may this poem be called? A prayer for guidance.

Stanza I

What are the poet's feelings? He feels very much depressed in spirit, as a traveller would who was far from home and alone in the gathering darkness.

Whom does he address as "Kindly Light"? Why does he use the term "Light"? He may remember that our Saviour called Himself "the Light of the world", and it is as his "Light" or Guide that the traveller feels his need of Him. He may be thinking of the Pillar of Fire and the Pillar of Cloud.

What image is suggested by the words "Lead, kindly Light"? It suggests something that has life (moves on before), and sheds a beneficent light on the travellers' path.

What is meant by the "gloom"? It means the condition of his mind. He is seeking Truth and feels that he cannot rely on reason alone to guide him.

What do the last two lines show about him? They show that he is humble and is content to be guided through the darkness "one step" at a time.

Stanza II

What more do we learn about his life in the second stanza? In what language is his former "pride" contrasted with his present humility? What is the meaning of "garish"? What part of his life is called "the garish day"? Why is it so called?

NOTE.—"Garish" means dazzling, and by "garish day" is meant the earlier care-free years when life seemed all brightness and the author felt perfectly certain of his ability to take care of himself.

What at times disturbed his life, even in those "past years"? What made him hide these fears? What is meant by saying "Pride ruled my will"? What now is his prayer concerning these years? Why does he want them put out of remembrance?

What is the relation of the second stanza to the first one? It contrasts the author's earlier attitude of mind toward God with what it is in later years, thus emphasizing the great change that has taken place in his life.

Compare the dependence depicted in the first stanza with the strength described in the second. In which case is the man really the stronger? Account for the fact that when he was strong, but not in his own strength, he really felt his weakness more than when he was weak.

NOTE.—The higher his ideal, the smaller he sees himself; and the lower his ideal, the larger he sees himself. Observe also how the prayer to be led "on" reveals the man's progressive spirit. The unprogressive man would pray simply for safety and protection.

Stanza III

What lesson does the poet learn from the "past years"? What confidence does this lesson give him for the future? What phases of experiences of life are suggested by "moor", "fen", "crag", and "torrent"?

NOTE.—To answer this, there should be an effort to image a moor, a fen, a crag, or a torrent clearly. Then when the pupil sees the desolate, lonesome moor; the miry, almost impassable fen; the sharp, out-jutting crag which makes the ascent more forbidding and difficult; and the rushing, unbridged torrent which must be forded or breasted, even though it threatens destruction; it should be easy to relate these to the experiences in life which they typify, or represent.

How long does the poet believe this guidance will last? In what words does he say that it will last as long as it will be needed? What does he mean by "the night"? Beyond "the night", what vision does he see? Whose are "those angel faces"?

What is the relation of the third stanza to the second? It shows how the author's confidence in the Divine guidance to be granted him during future years is strengthened by the lessons learned in former years.

The teacher should again read the poem aloud. This will impress upon the pupils, not only the truth and beauty of the poem, but also furnish an ideal to stimulate them in their preparation for the reading lesson which is to follow.

CHAPTER VII
FORM IV
ILLUSTRATIVE LESSONS

JUDAH'S SUPPLICATION TO JOSEPH

(Fourth Reader, page 51)

INTRODUCTION

Review briefly the Scriptural account of Joseph's life, and particularly the story of the visits of his brethren to Egypt to buy corn. Note especially the following points:

1. The famine in the land of Canaan; the first visit of Joseph's brothers to Egypt; their interview with Joseph; the detention of Simeon; Joseph's demand that Benjamin be brought down.

2. The return to Canaan; Jacob's refusal to let Benjamin go down into Egypt; Judah's becoming surety for his safe return.

3. The second visit of Joseph's brethren to Egypt, this time with Benjamin; their entertainment by Joseph; their homeward journey; the discovery of the silver cup in Benjamin's sack; their return to Joseph.

GENERAL ANALYSIS

After the selection has been read, the teacher should proceed by some such method as the following:

> With what does the passage deal? Judah's entreaty to Joseph for Benjamin's safe return to his father, and the effect it produced.
>
> Into how many parts is the selection naturally divided? Into three parts, corresponding to the paragraphs as given in the Reader.
>
> What is the principal idea in each part?
>
> 1. Joseph's decision to keep the offender as a bondman. (Paragraph I)
> 2. Judah's supplication to Joseph that Benjamin be permitted to return for his father's sake. (Paragraph II)
> 3. Joseph's revelation of his identity, and the provision he

makes for the maintenance of his kindred. (Paragraph III)

DETAILED ANALYSIS

Paragraph I

Why did Joseph's brethren fall "before him on the ground"? Prostration is the Eastern mode of signifying profound respect, complete submission.

What is the meaning of "divine"? In this sense, to look into the future; to see what is hidden from ordinary people.

Does Joseph claim explicitly to have this ability? No, he merely suggests it, probably to impress them with the idea of his power.

What does Judah mean by "the iniquity of thy servants"? Doubtless he has in mind the wrong that they committed years before, in selling Joseph to the Ishmaelites and deceiving their father. Verses 21 and 22 of the 42nd chapter of Genesis go to show that the consciousness of this sin was ever before them.

What was Judah's attitude toward the accusation brought against them? He frankly confesses the guilt of all—not of Benjamin only.

Why do you think he adopts this attitude, when he must have been sure that all were guiltless? He perhaps believes that they are victims of a conspiracy, the object of which is to place them in the power of this Egyptian governor, and he thinks that this submissive attitude is best calculated to secure mercy at his hands.

How do you account for Joseph's apparent desire to keep Benjamin in Egypt, with himself? Probably he thinks this the best means of inducing his father, Jacob, to come to Egypt. However, he may not really intend to keep Benjamin at all. He may be making the threat only to test Judah. It may be remembered that it was Judah who had counselled the selling of Joseph years before. Joseph may now be trying to see if Judah is the same kind of man he was when the selling into Egypt took place—whether he will sacrifice Benjamin in this extremity as he sacrificed Joseph himself.

If the latter is Joseph's object, how does the experiment succeed? It proves that Judah is a different man, that the years that have elapsed have produced a remarkable change in his character.

Paragraph II

Of what does Judah's entreaty largely consist? Of a recital of the governor's orders and of Jacob's attachment to Benjamin, the son in whom all the thoughts, hopes, and desires of his old age are centred.

Upon what does Judah lay the greatest emphasis? Upon the effect that Benjamin's detention will have upon his father. Evidently the brothers are very anxious to spare their father any unnecessary grief and pain.

For what purpose is the whole speech specially adapted? To stir the emotions. It is suited to appeal to the feelings of anybody, but, particularly, to the feelings of Egypt's governor, though his identity is still unknown.

Which are the most pathetic sentences? The two beginning with, "And we said unto my lord, We have a father, an old man", and "Now, therefore, when I come to thy servant, my father, and the lad be not with us".

What features of the speech would make the strongest appeal to Joseph? The reference to his father's old age and his attachment to Benjamin; his belief in Joseph's untimely end; the blow that separation from Benjamin would involve; Judah's willingness to sacrifice himself.

What light does the speech throw upon Judah's character? It shows a capacity for intense feeling, a deep devotion to his father, and a spirit of self-sacrifice. It might indicate also a shrewd knowledge of human nature, for he apparently knows how to present the case in the most effective manner.

What is the meaning of "thou art even as Pharaoh"? Thou art as mighty as the king of Egypt.

Explain "thy servant became surety for the lad unto my father". Judah had given Jacob a guarantee that Benjamin should return safely.

Select any figurative expression and give its meaning. "Thy servants shall bring down the gray hairs of thy servant our father with sorrow to the grave." The blow which separation from Benjamin would involve will cause the aged father to die of a broken heart.

What are the main characteristics of the supplication? The language is simple and direct, the feeling is of the loftiest character, and the whole speech is highly eloquent. If the test of true eloquence is the intensity of the appeal it makes to worthy emotions, this passage may well be regarded as one of the most eloquent in all literature.

Paragraph III

Did Joseph purposely select this as the most fitting moment to reveal himself? No. He revealed himself because he could not help it and because Judah's appeal had so worked upon his feelings. The first sentence of the paragraph indicates this.

Why did he send every man away except his brothers? He did not wish others to see his own lack of self-control or his brothers' shame and embarrassment. Moreover, it was a solemn situation, too sacred for vulgar eyes to gaze upon.

We are told that he "wept aloud", that "he fell upon his brother Benjamin's neck, and wept", that "he kissed all his brethren", etc. Is he unduly demonstrative? Eastern people are much more emotional and demonstrative than Western people.

Why did he have to repeat his assurance that he was Joseph? The first announcement was so amazing that it seemed incredible to them. Moreover, all his previous communications had been through an interpreter and, no doubt, their amazement was increased by hearing him address them in their own tongue.

Upon what ground did Joseph tell his brothers that they should not blame themselves for selling him into Egypt? Upon the ground that God had brought good out of the evil they had done.

Is he quite right in telling them that they should not be grieved for the wrong they did him? They were free agents; God did not will that they should sin, though He brought good out of it. From this point of view Joseph is wrong. But he doubtless sees that his brothers have long ago repented their action and does not wish them to continue to blame themselves. His assurance is no doubt prompted by a noble generosity induced, to some extent, by Judah's appeal.

What seems to be Joseph's dominating motive? His love for his father. His repeated references to him show this.

We can understand his desire to provide for his father and Benjamin, but why for his brothers who had wronged him? Partly for his father's sake, perhaps. It was natural, in those patriarchal days, that Jacob, if he migrated to Egypt, should wish his family to do the same. Besides, Joseph sees that his brothers are changed men.

What inducements does he hold out to them? He shows them that his own power in Egypt is sufficient to protect them; he promises them the fertile land of Goshen, with sufficient food for themselves and their flocks and herds; and he points out that five years of famine are yet to be in the land, and that they must inevitably suffer if the invitation is rejected.

Joseph frequently draws attention to his power in Egypt. Is he at all vain-glorious? No, he does this to assure his brothers that the wrong done him years before has had, through the goodness of God, a beneficent result; to show them that it has not been all suffering in his long exile; and to induce his father to come down to Egypt.

"After that his brethren talked with him." About what would they probably talk? No doubt Joseph would ask many things about what had occurred in Canaan since he left, and would give his brothers an account of his own experiences in Egypt.

Does it not seem strange that Joseph, during all these years, should never have taken measures to find out how his kindred fared, or to assure them that he was still alive? He was probably ever looking forward to such a situation as this, confident that the dreams of his boyhood would still be realized. It was, perhaps, this belief in the ultimate fulfilment of his dreams that had kept him silent during these years.

What qualities of character does Joseph show in his speech? A spirit of noble generosity and forgiveness, filial devotion, and a desire to find good in the midst of seeming evil.

Point out passages that indicate these qualities. What admirable characteristics does the whole selection exhibit? Simplicity, directness, and eloquence of language, noble emotion, loftiness of character, and high ideals.

As a final synthesis of the lesson, let the pupils tell the story in their own words, preserving, as far as possible, the same order of ideas as is followed in the extract. This will reveal to the teacher whether they have grasped the ideas in their proper relationship.

MERCY

(Fourth Reader, page 89)

THE SETTING OF THE SELECTION

This selection is taken from Shakespeare's play *The Merchant of Venice,* iv. i. In this play, Shylock, a Jew of Venice, had loaned Antonio three thousand ducats, repayable on a certain date without interest, but if not so paid, Antonio was to forfeit a pound of flesh from such part of his body as pleased the Jew. Antonio, not being able to pay the money as agreed, Shylock sued for the fulfilment of the bond, and in court refused to accept even three times the amount borrowed, insisting on a pound of the merchant's flesh. According to the law, there appeared to be no help for Antonio, but the judge, Portia, asked Shylock to show mercy. To this he answered, "On what compulsion must I? Tell me that." This selection is part of Portia's reply to Shylock's question. The teacher should relate to the pupils the outline given above.

ANALYSIS OF THE THOUGHT

1. The qualities of mercy:
   (1) It is not forced.
   (2) It is gentle.
   (3) It carries a twofold blessing.
   (4) It is the most powerful attribute in men of might.
   (5) It is divine in its nature.
2. Where mercy is found:
   (1) It is found "enthroned in the hearts of kings".
   (2) It is found as a Divine attribute.
3. The results of showing mercy:
   (1) It adds strength to strength.
   (2) It makes man God-like.

Question, in order to develop the analysis of the thought, and write on the board the topics, as given by the pupils.

THE DIFFICULTIES

Quality of mercy. The nature of mercy is not strained, is not forced. When the Jew asks "Upon what compulsion must I?", Portia answers that compulsion has nothing to do with mercy. It is not in the nature of mercy to be a result of compulsion.

Mightiest in the mightiest. This is capable of a double interpretation—(1) the quality of mercy in a man of great power must be strong in proportion as his power is great. (2) Mercy is at its greatest when exhibited by the greatest. Portia would wish to convey the first meaning, as that would have the more weight with Shylock.

Becomes the thronèd monarch. The possession of this quality makes a man more truly kingly than the mere wearing of a crown.

Sceptre. The symbol of the monarch's authority.

Temporal power. Power which belongs to this world only.

Mercy—is enthronèd in the hearts of kings. The "hearts of kings" are for mercy what the throne itself is for a king—the most exalted position he can occupy.

Mercy seasons justice. Mercy tempers justice, rendering it less severe and making it more acceptable and pleasing.

Develop the meaning through Illustration, when possible. For example, to teach the meaning of "seasons" in "mercy seasons justice", lead the pupils to use the word seasons in such sentences as: We season our food with spices. Lead, from the meaning in common or familiar use, to its use in the lesson. Avoid mere dictionary meanings of words. Teach the use of the word where it is found, never one of its meanings apart from its use.

THE ARGUMENT

There is no compulsion in mercy. Its course is always from the higher to the lower. It is a blessing to both giver and receiver. The greater the mercy shown, the greater will be the giver. To show mercy does more to make a monarch kingly than does his crown. The one stands for the exercise of authority and power commanding obedience and awe; the other comes from the heart and reveals the character. It is more than kingly, it is God-like; for in exercising it, man's power becomes more like God's than in any other way.

Develop the above argument by questioning. Sum up the result by requiring the whole argument to be given by a pupil orally in his own language. Finally, require the pupils to write, as forcibly as they can, the whole of Portia's argument.

The remainder of Portia's speech as given in the play may also be given to the pupils. In that case, the remainder of the argument should be given as follows:

You demand justice, Jew. Even so, require it as you hope Heaven may require it of you. Consider that mercy is necessary to salvation, and remember that, as we all pray for mercy, that fact itself requires us all to show the deeds of mercy.

The speech containing this part of the argument is as follows:

> Therefore, Jew,
> Though justice be thy plea, consider this,
> That, in the course of justice, none of us
> Should see salvation: We do pray for mercy;
> And that same prayer doth teach us all to render
> The deeds of mercy.

"We do pray for mercy", refers to the general prayer of humanity for mercy. To have limited its reference to the petition for mercy in the Lord's Prayer would have weakened its force to the Jew.

MORNING ON THE LIÈVRE

(Fourth Reader, page 228)

ASSIGNMENT

1. The teacher should explain to the pupils that the Lièvre River (pronounced Lee-eh-vr) runs through a deep gorge in the height of land on the Quebec side of the Ottawa River, into which it flows not far from the Capital. In some places, the banks of the Lièvre rise abruptly to a great height; at others more gradually, the slope being covered with a thick forest growth. As the river nears the Ottawa, the banks become much lower. The scenery, whether viewed from the height above or from the river below, is very beautiful.

2. The teacher should ask a few questions which can be answered easily from the pupil's own reading of the poem, for example:

From what position does the author first view the scene? What things in the scene appeal to each of the pupils as the most beautiful? Describe the incident mentioned in the last stanza. State in a single sentence the subject-matter of the whole poem.

TREATMENT

The pupils' answers to the questions given when the lesson was assigned should be dealt with first.

Stanza I

> What first attracts the author's attention as he looks upward? What makes us feel how high up the banks the mist extends? What part of the mist appears most beautiful? Why? To what is it compared? How does this comparison affect our impression of (1) the colour of the mist; (2) the height of the mist? Does the comparison make the meaning clearer? Is the comparison apt? Is it beautiful?

NOTE.—When a blacksmith cools the red-hot iron in a tub of water, vapour rises to the roof of his shop. The blaze from his forge shining on this mist produces the colours mentioned. The amethyst is a precious stone, clear and translucent, with a colour inclining to purple. The presence of coal dust or smoke in the vapour would help to produce the colour of amethyst. The same effect would result, if some smoke or dust were mingled with the mist where the sun's rays reach it at the top of the gorge.

> "Screams his matins to the day." What is meant? What idea does the author wish to convey by this mention of the bird? Out of hearing "of the clang of his hammer" gives a strong impression of the great height of the gorge. Of what "giant" are we made to think? What is meant by "skirts of mist"?

The teacher's reading of this stanza, a part at a time, if it is taken up in that way, or all at once, should aid much in impressing upon the minds of the pupils the wonderful beauty of the scene described, and this is the main purpose of the lesson.

Stanza II

The author is paddling down the river. Describe the movement. What shows that the mist has risen from the surface of the water? What indicates the calmness of the river? What things connected with himself does the author show to be in harmony with the scene? How does he indicate the harmony in each of the following: The motion of his canoe, the surface of the water, his own activity, the force of gravity, the character of the morning, and the forest life? We should expect him to dip his paddle very quietly, if he felt the calmness of the morning, but to show that the "silence" pervades all nature, the very drops of water from the paddle blades seem to fall gently, in sympathy with the spirit of silence reigning all around. What are the "river reaches"? The reach is the stretch of the river between two bends. How are they "borne in a mirror"? The high cliff-like banks are mirrored in the surface of the water. Explain the colour "purple gray". It is the colour of the image of the banks in the water. What is meant by "sheer away"? It means that the "river reaches" curve away like a winding road. Try to see the picture of the winding river, apparently growing smaller as it passes curve after curve. As it seems to recede into the distance, the surface of the river forms a "misty line of light", just before it melts into the shadows of the forest. Where do the forest and the stream seem to meet? What does the word "plight" suggest about their meeting? What suggests a meeting-place out of sight? Why is the meeting represented as taking place in the shadow? Now what is described in the second stanza?

"As a cloud", "like a dream". Do these make the meaning clearer? Explain. Are these comparisons apt? Show the fitness of "silvery", "crystal deep", "asleep".

Stanza III

As the author goes farther and farther down the stream, the river runs more slowly. How is this shown? What shows that the little creek runs very slowly into the river? How does the author say the creek is winding? Why would not the same word "curling" do to show that the river was winding through the gorge? What are we told about the mouth of the creek? See those sunken wrecks down in the water. What are they like? What shows you that they are very large tree trunks? What starts the ducks? See them as they rise out of the water. Make a drawing to show their position. The drawing should show them flying in the shape of a horizontal letter V, as wild ducks fly. What words show you that they keep this position unbroken? Hear them as they fly off at their utmost speed. Why such haste? What makes the "swivelling whistle"? This is the noise they make as they fly. Imagine a whistle to be set whirling around as it whistles. The change in the sound due to the whirling motion of the whistle might be called a swivelling whistle. See them go, led through the shadow. Hear them, as they disappear behind a rocky point ahead. What is meant by their "whirr"? What has made us forget all about the beauty of the silent morning? What effect did this silence probably have on the poet's judgment of the noise made by the ducks? Now what is described in the third stanza?

Consider the fitness of the words "lazy", "sucks", "bleeds", "sneak", "swept", "splashy".

SYNTHESIS OF THE WHOLE BY CORRELATING THE LESSON WITH ART

1. Make a sketch of the scene in the first stanza, showing the rocky, high, forest-covered banks, with mist rising along the slopes, and the man in a canoe on a small stream below.

2. Make a sketch of the scene described in the second stanza, showing the winding river, with its high banks appearing to meet in the distance, the man in his canoe in the foreground, and over all the dim light of early morning.

3. Make a sketch of the ducks rising from the water. Show the reeds at the mouth of the creek and the rocky spur toward which the birds are heading.

THE LIFE OF THE AUTHOR

As it is not necessary to know anything about the author to fully understand this poem, nothing should be said about his life until the pupils become interested in him through their interest in what he has written. Then teach the main points in his life. See sketch of his life, at the back of the Manual on *The Ontario Readers*.

DICKENS IN THE CAMP

(Fourth Reader, page 287)

INTRODUCTION

By way of introduction, it might be well to tell the pupils something of Bret Harte—his residence in California, his experience as a prospector in the goldfields, his stories of the mining camps, and his admiration of Dickens. (See Manual on *The Ontario Readers*, p. 315.) These facts throw considerable light upon the poem, and will be useful in aiding the pupils to interpret it properly. This poem was written shortly after the death of Dickens. It might well follow the study of *David Copperfield's First Journey Alone* and *The Indignation of Nicholas Nickleby.*

PREPARATION

When the poem has been read, the teacher should, before beginning the analysis, ask a few general questions, such as:

What has Dickens to do with the story related in the poem? He was the author of the book read in the camp, *Old Curiosity Shop*, of which "Nell" is the heroine. (A brief outline of the story, with special reference to the feelings it arouses in the reader, might be given here.)

What kind of camp is referred to in the poem? A mining camp. The last line of the second stanza suggests this.

Where is the scene laid? Apparently in California, among the Sierra Nevada Mountains. This is indicated in the first stanza.

What is the leading idea of the poem? The effect which the reading of a story by Dickens produced in a Western mining camp.

What are the main sub-topics?

1. The scene of the incident. Stanzas I-III.
2. The reading of the story. Stanzas IV-VII.
3. A lament for the death of Dickens. Stanzas VIII-X.

MINUTE ANALYSIS

Stanza I

How does the description of the scene, as given in stanza I, differ from that given in stanza II? Stanza I gives the background and the remote surroundings, while stanza II places us in the midst of the camp.

What features give the story a romantic setting? The stately "pines", the singing "river", the "slowly drifting moon", the snow-capped mountains.

From the description in the first stanza, give as clear a picture of the location of the camp as possible. It was situated on the edge of a cañon in the Sierras, towering pines rising round about, the river flowing noisily beneath, and the mountains uplifting their snow-covered peaks in the distance.

Explain the comparison suggested in the last two lines. The mountain summits, with their everlasting snows, resemble in the distance the minarets, or lofty tapering towers, attached to Mohammedan mosques.

Which is preferable, "minarets of snow", or "snow-covered

peaks"? The former, because it is a more unusual expression and because of what it suggests.

Stanza II

Why is the camp-fire represented as a rude humorist? It causes faces and forms that are haggard and care-worn to appear fresh and healthy, thus playing a grim jest upon those gathered round it.

Explain the significance of "fierce" in the last line. In the mad rush for gold, all the worst elements of man's nature are brought to the surface—disregard for the rights of others, contempt for law and order, and even carelessness with regard to human life.

Consider the fitness of the words "rude", "painted", "race", as used here.

Stanza III

What indicates the value that the owner places upon this book? The words "treasure" and "hoarded" suggest that it is one of his most highly prized possessions.

What suggests that this is not the first time the story has been read in camp? The word "anew".

How does the poet indicate the absorbing interest that the story has for these men? He says the fascination is so great as to draw the attention of these rough miners even from their card-playing. Explain "listless leisure".

Stanza IV

Explain "the firelight fell". The fire gradually died down, because, absorbed in their interest in the story, the miners forgot to put on fresh fuel.

Why is Dickens called the "Master"? A master is one who attains the highest degree of skill in some art. Dickens was master of the art of story-telling, a master of vivid narration, a master of pathos and humour.

Stanzas V and VI

Is there anything in these stanzas which might throw light upon the identity of the reader? He is probably the poet himself. His familiarity with the fancies of the reader seem to indicate this. Besides, the reader is kept very much in the background—we are told only that he was young—and this seems to be in keeping with the modesty of the poet as shown elsewhere in the poem. At any rate, we must admit that the reader was a poet, for he indulges in fancies of a highly poetical nature.

What are those fancies? Such is the absorbing interest of the story that even the pines and cedars seem to stand silent to listen, and the fir trees gather closer in order that nothing may escape their hearing.

What is the poetic element in these fancies? Ascribing to inanimate objects the power of human interest and sympathy.

What effect does the poet secure by picturing the trees as listeners? It enhances our idea of the absorbing interest of the story.

Mention any other illustrations of a poet's use of this device of attributing human sympathies to inanimate objects. Many might be given, for example:

Byron's *Waterloo:*

> And Ardennes waves above them her green leaves,
> Dewy with Nature's tear-drops, as they pass,
> Grieving, if aught inanimate e'er grieves,
> Over the unreturning brave.

Longfellow's *Evangeline* describing the song of the mocking-bird:

> Shook from his little throat such floods of delirious music,
> That the whole air and the woods and waves seemed silent to listen.

Mrs. Hemans' *The Landing of the Pilgrim Fathers:*

> Amidst the storm they sang, and the stars heard, and the sea.

What experience of "Nell" is alluded to in the last two lines of stanza V? She and her grandfather had been lost on their journey from London.

Why does the poet say that the whole camp "lost their way" with "Nell" on English meadows? The narrative was so vivid that the miners, in spirit, accompanied her in her wanderings.

Stanza VII

What is meant by "Their cares dropped from them"? They forgot themselves, their cares and privations, and realized the hopes and fears, the joys and sorrows of "Little Nell".

How was this result brought about? It was due to the fascination of the story.

To what does the poet compare this? To some "spell divine", some supernatural influence, which causes their own troubles to disappear for the time being.

Give, then, the meaning of "o'ertaken as by some spell divine". They are brought, as it were, under the influence of some magician, who, by the exercise of his power, transports them from their own world to that in which "Nell" lives and moves.

Show the beauty of the comparison in the last two lines of this stanza. As the needles of the pine, through the action of the wind, fall silently and almost unperceived, so the cares of the miners were forgotten in the all-compelling interest of the story.

Compare Longfellow:

> The cares that infest the day
> Shall fold their tents like the Arabs,
> And as silently steal away.

Why is this comparison more appropriate than, for example, like the leaves from the trees in autumn, or, like snow-flakes from the clouds in winter? Because it is drawn from the objects at hand, not from more remote things—an example of local colour.

Explain "gusty pine". A pine exposed to the mountain blasts.

Stanza VIII

Who is referred to by "he" in the second line? Dickens—not the reader of the story.

What is meant by "wrought that spell"? Produced that magic influence.

State the question in full. Is "he who wrought that spell" lost, too?

What tale has the "towering pine" to tell? That the mining camp has disappeared.

And what the "stately Kentish spire"? That Dickens has gone. (Dickens' home was at Gadshill, in Kent.)

What is the one tale that both have to tell? A tale of disappearance and death.

Is the question asked in the second line answered? Not directly, though the answer is implied.

State the substantial meaning of the stanza. The "towering pine" of the Sierras tells of the disappearance of the mining camp; the "stately spire" of Kent tells of the death of Dickens; both bear witness to the potent influence of Dickens.

Stanza IX

What is the "fragrant story" of the Western mining camp? The tribute that the incident related in the poem pays to the magical power of Dickens as a story writer.

Why is it called a "fragrant story"? The author poetically conceives of it as being laden with the fragrance of the fir, the pine, and the cedar—a sort of "incense" to the memory of the "Master".

What is incense? The odours of spices and gums burned in religious rites.

What poetic idea does the author express in the last two lines? The hopvines of Kent are represented as uniting with the pine, fir, and cedar in sending forth their fragrance as incense.

What is the meaning, then, of the whole stanza? Let the fragrance of the pine, the cedar, and the fir, mingled with the odours of the Kentish hopvines, be as incense to the memory of the "Master".

Stanza X

Does the poet mean that the grave of Dickens is literally adorned with oak, holly, and laurel wreaths? No; he is speaking figuratively.

What do these typify? The tributes of admiration, reverence, and love that are paid to the memory of Dickens in his own country.

Of what is each emblematic? The oak is emblematic of England, the life of whose people he so vividly depicted; the holly suggests his charming Christmas stories; the laurel signifies his mastery of the art of writing.

What does the poet mean by "This spray of Western pine"? This poem was written in the Western World, as a tribute to the memory of the great novelist.

What personal characteristic does the poet show in the third line? A sense of humility, which leads him to suggest that this poem is unworthy of a place among the tributes paid to the name and fame of the great artist.

Stripped of its figurative significance, what is the meaning of the whole stanza? To the many tokens of love and admiration that are offered to the memory of Dickens, may I be permitted to add this poem—a Western tribute to the worldwide influence of the famous author.

RECONSTRUCTION

Tell the story of the poem in your own words.

In a cañon of the Sierras, a group of rough miners were gathered about a camp-fire. Around them stood the stately pines, above which the moon was slowly rising; below, at the bottom of the cañon, a river sang, as it threaded its way among the boulders; and, far in the distance, the mountains reared their snow-covered summits to the evening sky. The flickering camp-fire played strange tricks upon those gathered round it, for it gave to the care-worn faces and bent forms of the miners the appearance of freshness and health.

One of the miners, a mere youth, opened his pack, drew therefrom a copy of Dickens' *Old Curiosity Shop*, and began to read aloud. At once, all other occupations were suspended, and everybody drew near to listen to the story. The whole camp yielded itself to the fascination of the tale, and in its absorbing interest they forgot themselves and their surroundings, their ills, their hardships, and their cares. One might almost fancy that the very pines and cedars became silent, and that the fir trees drew closer to hear the story of "Little Nell".

Dickens, the "Master", has gone, but, among the many tributes that are paid to his power as a writer, let this little tale of the Western camp be added, to illustrate the universal nature of his influence.

DOST THOU LOOK BACK ON WHAT HATH BEEN

(Fourth Reader, page 289)

PREPARATION

This lesson should be preceded by a suitable preparatory lesson on the life of some man, for example, Peel, Disraeli, or Lincoln, who, in spite of all obstacles, rose to eminence in the nation and lived "To mould a mighty state's decrees".

INTRODUCTION

Tennyson and Arthur Hallam, as young men at college, were great friends. The bond of affection between them was probably as strong as it was possible for friendship between two men to be. When Hallam died in 1833, at twenty-two years of age, Tennyson said of him: "He was as near perfection as a mortal man could be". From time to time during the next seventeen years, Tennyson wrote short poems on themes which occurred to him in connection with his thoughts of Hallam. These he finally collected and published in one volume, called *In Memoriam*.

PURPOSE

The purpose of this lesson should be in harmony with the purpose of *In Memoriam*. It should, therefore, be a study of life within the comprehension of the pupils. The lesson should aid in securing the development of character and an appreciation of worthy ambition and enduring friendship.

ASSIGNMENT

The lesson should be assigned in such a way as to encourage the pupils' natural desire to learn something through their own efforts. A few questions should be given to be answered from their own study, for example:

1. What does the first line show regarding Tennyson's present thought of Hallam?
2. What stanzas describe the progress of the man who reminds him of Hallam?
3. What is described in the remaining stanzas?
4. What lines suggest something about this man's feelings toward the scenes and friends of his youth?
5. In what respect, according to the last stanza, does Tennyson show that one of these old-time friends is like himself?

CLASS WORK

What does Tennyson describe in the first four stanzas?

Stanza I

Why does he call the man "divinely gifted"? Because he has had great natural gifts.

When should we call a man of only ordinary ability "divinely gifted"? What have you read that illustrates this? (If the pupils cannot answer this question, the teacher should tell briefly the parable of the talents.)

What is meant by "Whose life in low estate began"? Why are the details about his early life mentioned? State briefly the thought contained in this stanza.

Stanza II

What was the effect of his humble birth on his progress in early life? In what ways did it act as a bar: (1) upon his own mind; (2) upon the good-will of others toward himself? Which of these two do the following lines from *Œnone* indicate that the poet would say must be overcome first?

> Self-reverence, self-knowledge, self-control,
> These three alone lead life to sovereign power.

State in your own words, the full meaning of "breaks his birth's invidious bar". NOTE.—"Invidious" means likely to incur, or bring on envy, ill-will, or hatred.

What idea is suggested in the second line as to the opportunities which come to such a man? Imagine him grasping these fleeting chances. What were his probable feelings toward those things which eluded his grasp? (Be careful in answering this. Remember that the man has gained the mastery of himself.)

What is meant by "blows of circumstance"? What were some of these difficulties?

What does the action-word "breasts" suggest: (1) about the character of these difficulties, (2) about the character of the man? Explain "grapples with his evil star". What is the allusion? Tell, in the poet's own words, what this "evil star" was. Imagine this man grappling with it. What term do boys often use for a similar action? Which is going to win this wrestling match? Give reasons, from what the man has already done, for thinking that he will win. What does this action show about his belief in luck?

What do the action-words in this stanza suggest about the man's character? What sounds in each of the words help to emphasize this grim determination?

State briefly the relation of the thought of this stanza to that of the first.

Stanza III

What effect did the man's early struggles have on his mental power and character? What does Tennyson call this increased energy and strength of character? He calls it "force". Now, explain "makes by force his merit known".

What position in the gift of the nation do the next three lines show that he gained at last? What words indicate the emblem of the Premier's power?

"Clutch the golden keys." What does this action suggest as to his character? What word is generally used to denote such determination to gain power and influence? What makes such ambition lawful? What use does Tennyson show this man made of his ambition? What is meant by "mould a mighty state's decrees"? As Premier, to whom would it be his duty to give advice?

The people know that the sovereign must act on the advice of his ministers, of whom the Premier is the most influential; but they believe that the judgment of the sovereign often modifies and improves this advice. To the nation, this influence of the sovereign is a silent force, but, like the silent forces in nature, they believe it to be powerful.

In what words does Tennyson express this mutual influence of the King and the Premier? What features of this influence are expressed respectively by the words "shape" and "whisper"? What action-words in this stanza suggest the relation (1) of effort,

(2) of time, to the magnitude of the work?

State in a single sentence the thought of this stanza.

Stanza IV

What is the final test of the value of a law? Its effects on the people. In what words does Tennyson show the effect on the people of the laws made through this man's influence?

Explain how this man became "The pillar of a people's hope". What words show the far-reaching extent of his influence? Which shows the more force in the man, his influence with the King or his later influence in the whole nation? In what words does Tennyson show which he thinks the greater? To which do "high" and "higher" respectively refer? What does "Fortune's crowning slope" suggest about (1) the honour which the man has now gained, (2) the nature of the road he has travelled?

Stanza V

Picture the man as he looks back after having reached the height of his ambition. Describe his mood. At what times does he indulge in these dreamy memories? What does he seem to see in these quiet hours? What hill and stream does the poet mean? What feeling does each awaken? Why is the "sweetness" called "secret"? Why is the "dearness" called "distant"?

Stanza VI

What part of his life is meant by "his narrower fate"? With what is he comparing that early life, when he calls it "his narrower fate"? Using similar language, what might his present position of great influence be called?

Some think that the first line of this stanza refers to the limitations or restrictions of his early life, while others say the poet was thinking simply of the stream, as the limit or boundary of the things that influenced his childhood. Which view is to be preferred? Which meaning agrees with the use of the word "its" in the next line? Would this man now look back on those difficulties of his early life as limitations and hindrances, or as things which helped to make him what he is?

Now explain "The limit of his narrower fate". Compare the direction in which he looks in his day dreams now, with the direction in which he looked in those of his boyhood. What is meant by "vocal springs"?

In what way were the games of his youth prophetic of his future work as a man? What do people mean by saying, "The boy is father of the man"?

Stanza VII

Describe the present occupation of the friend of his boyhood. What information about his friend does the word "native" give us? What phrases show how he does his work?

Compare the farmer's query in the last line with that in the first line of the poem.

SYNOPSIS OF DETAILS

Under the following heads, point out the resemblance of Hallam to the statesman and of Tennyson to the farmer:

1. Early friendship
2. Their separation
3. Progress since parting
4. Memories of each other.

It is hoped that no teacher will use these questions as a substitute for his own questioning. If they are accepted as suggestive in regard to both interpretation and method, they may be of real service, otherwise they will be almost valueless.

WATERLOO

(Fourth Reader, page 311)

AIM

To lead the pupils to appreciate the music and imagery of the poem.

PREPARATION

Where is Waterloo situated? In Belgium. What two armies were engaged in this battle? The French and the English; with the latter were some Prussian allies. Who were the French and the English commanders? Napoleon and Wellington. What was the result of the battle? The overthrow of Napoleon and his banishment to St. Helena. What would have been the consequence if Wellington had been defeated? Napoleon would possibly have had complete mastery of Europe. Picture this struggle of great commanders and disciplined armies, while Europe waited breathlessly for the outcome. (The pupils should read some good history of this battle.)

PRESENTATION

Read the poem to the pupils in such a way as to make vivid the scenes depicted.

DEVELOPMENT

What has the poet described in this poem? Some of the events preceding the battle.

What are the main pictures found in each stanza? (Write on the black-board.)

1. The ball
2. The sound of the enemy's cannon
3. The Duke of Brunswick
4. The farewells
5. The muster
6. The gathering of the Highlanders
7. The march to battle
8. Summary of pictures and the result.

Do you see any stanza that interferes with the progress of the action? The third stanza anticipates the battle and destroys the continuity between the sounds of the approaching enemy and the hurried farewells.

Why does the poet devote a special stanza to the Highlanders? Were they more worthy of mention than the English and Irish regiments? The author, George Gordon, Lord Byron, belonged to a Scotch family. The muster of the Highlanders at midnight, combined with their stirring music, made a very picturesque incident.

Consider the elements which contribute to the various scenes:

Stanza I

What is described? The ball given by the Duchess of Richmond. What is the emotion of this stanza? Pleasure, gaiety. What is the picture in the first line? The arrival of the guests, the welcomes, and the "revelry" of the assembly. Why does the author say "Belgium's capital" rather than "Brussels"? It suggests the capital of a nation with a noble people. Who were the "Beauty" and the "Chivalry"? The ladies, the officers of the army, and the nobility. Describe the picture you see in "bright the lamps shone o'er fair women and brave men". The large ball-room, the brilliantly lighted chandeliers, the beautiful costumes of the ladies, the uniforms and decorations of officers and nobles. Describe the images that are suggested by "and when music arose with its voluptuous swell". The bands of the regiments are playing the music of the dance. Notice how the poet changes the rhythm to the foot of three syllables, to indicate the music of the waltz. What contrast do you find in the last two lines? "Marriage bell" and "rising knell". What was the purpose of this? To show the contrast between pleasure and fear.

Stanza II

What is the theme? The sound of the enemy's cannon. Why does the author use the dramatic form? A conversation between two people of opposite temperaments gives greater reality to the picture. The first seems to expect danger, but is, for a moment, silenced by the other's upbraiding him for attempting to spoil the pleasure of the evening. A repetition of the "heavy sound" proves that he is right. The second is a lover of pleasure, who would not have the first speaker alarm the guests by his gloomy anticipations. Show how the second speaker indicates his impatience. His answers are short, he speaks in ellipses. "On with the dance", and "No sleep till morn". Notice the positive tone of the first speaker in the repetition, "It is—it is".

Stanza III

What is described here? The fate of Brunswick? Why does the author single out Brunswick from all the others who died? One specific case appeals to the reader more effectually than the report of the death of unknown thousands. Brunswick's father had been a noted general in the war with Napoleon. Explain, "Death's prophetic ear". This refers to a common superstition that "the veil of the future is lifted to those near to death". Show how the poet has broken the order of succession of the pictures. Brunswick's death is recorded before the breaking up of the ball is described.

Stanza IV

What is the theme? The farewells. What is the emotion? Fear and anguish. What words show this? "Gathering tears", "tremblings of distress", "cheeks all pale", "sudden partings", etc. Give a line in a preceding stanza that expresses the same thought as "mutual eyes". "Soft eyes looked love to eyes which spake again."

Stanza V

What is described? The muster of the troops. What is the prevailing feeling? The haste of the soldiers and the terror of the citizens. How does the poet show this haste? By the use of such phrases as "hot haste", "mustering squadron", "clattering car", "impetuous speed", "swiftly forming", as well as by the rapid movement of the verse. Why did the citizens of Brussels fear, since they had not to fight? They dreaded the pillage and ruin which would follow a French victory. Describe the scene in your own words—the cavalry forming in line, the movements of the artillery, the noise of distant cannon, the "alarming drum", and the panic of the citizens.

Stanza VI

The gathering of the Highlanders. Does the poet address the ear or the eye in this description? Only the sound of the bagpipes is described, though it may suggest a picture of the Highland regiments. What words describe the music? "Wild and high", "war-note", "thrills savage and shrill". Why does the poet mention proper names—"Lochiel", "Evan", "Donald"? The bagpipes recall stirring memories of these men, which inspire the clansmen to prove worthy of their ancestors. What is the "Cameron's gathering"? The war-song of the Cameron clan. Were there only Camerons in the Highland regiments? No, the Camerons were only one famous clan, but are taken here as representative of the heroism of all the Highlanders. Again, the use of individual specific cases produces a greater impression than a more general term. What was the "pibroch"? A wild, irregular species of music played on the bagpipes, adapted particularly to rouse a martial spirit among troops going to battle.

Stanza VII

What is described in this stanza? The march to the battle-field. What words show that? "As they pass". They were going through the forest of "Ardennes". What is the mood of this stanza? Sadness. The trees are represented as shedding tears when "Nature" thinks of the sad fate awaiting so many brave men. What were those tears? The expression refers to the dew of the early morning on the leaves of the trees, but the poet has called it "Nature's tear-drops". It is only a fanciful presentation of a natural phenomenon. Explain, "if aught inanimate e'er grieves". If inanimate nature, such as trees or grass, can express sorrow. Nature cannot grieve, but we appreciate the beauty of the imagery. Point out a contrast in this stanza. "This fiery mass of living valour", and "shall moulder cold and low".

Stanza VIII

What is the purpose of this stanza? It gives a summary of the preceding ones. Which stanza corresponds to line 2? Stanza I. Which corresponds to line 3? Stanzas II, III, and IV. Which stanzas picture the "marshalling in arms"? Stanzas V and VI. What stanzas picture "Battle's magnificently stern array"? Stanzas V and VII. Now contrast all these pictures with the last. The story is epitomized, and the end described—"friend, foe,—in one red burial blent!"

The pupils should now read the poem, in order that the teacher may judge by the varying tones and movements whether it has been properly appreciated.

THREE SCENES IN THE TYROL

(Fourth Reader, page 336)

AIM

To lead the pupils to appreciate the thrilling pictures and to understand the means by which the author has produced this vividness.

PREPARATION

The pupils have been required to read this lesson at their seats or at home.

Where is the Tyrol situated? It is a province in the Austrian Alps directly east of Switzerland. (Show its position on the map.)

The mountains are majestic, high, precipitous; the people daring and independent. The Tyrol is noted for the many accidents which happen to mountain-climbers. Who are the chief persons concerned in these three scenes? Maximilian I, Charles V, and Napoleon.

The author wishes to give, amid the most impressive surroundings, three stirring events in the lives of three great Emperors. State briefly the first story. The Emperor Maximilian was hunting a chamois, when he slipped on the edge of the precipice, rolled helplessly over, and caught a jutting ledge of rock, which interrupted his descent. An outlaw hastened to his assistance and guided him to safety.

PRESENTATION

I

Yes, this story is often called "The Rescue". Let us note how the author helps us to see the picture. Where does he place the spectator? On a "thread-like road" running between the rocky bank of the Inn River and the foot of the precipice of the Solstein.

What does the author ask you, as the imaginary spectator, to do? To throw your head back and look upward.

Why? The precipice towers perpendicularly many hundred feet above you. He wishes you to imagine you are standing on this road and the scene is taking place before your eyes.

What do you see? A hunter in pursuit of a chamois.

Describe this hunter. He is lofty and chivalrous in his bearing.

What happens? He is bounding on after a chamois toward the

edge of a precipice, when he loses his footing and falls.

How does the author make you see this plainly? He uses the present tense, as if the scene were happening now—"is bounding", "loses his footing", "rolls helplessly".

Any other way? Yes, he utters exclamations, "Mark!" "Ah!" Every act is told in the form of an exclamation.

"What is it that arrests him?" This is a question. Does the author expect an answer? No, he asks the question as I would ask it of myself if I saw the hunter stopped in his descent.

Why does he not tell you who this hunter is? I see now for the first time that it is the great Emperor Maximilian who is in such peril.

Does any one else see him? Yes, the Abbot, or head of a neighbouring monastery.

Why does the author mention him? To indicate that, apparently, human aid could not save the Emperor.

What has been told us in this first paragraph? The peril of the Emperor.

What is told us in the next? His rescue.

Who else sees the danger? Zyps of Zirl.

Who is he? A famous hunter and outlaw.

Do you see him at first? No, I hear his cry. The author says "Hark! there is a wild cry!" Then I recognize the outlaw.

Why does he utter the cry? To encourage the Emperor and let him know there is some one coming to his rescue.

Again how does the author make the picture vivid? By the use of the present tense, by commands, questions, and exclamations, and by making the spectator, in his excitement, address the mountaineer directly; for example, "thou hunted and hunting outlaw, art thou out upon the heights?" etc.

By what means does the author show how the outlaw comes to the Emperor's aid? By comparing him with the chamois, the insect, and the squirrel. This man combines in himself all their powers of movement.

What does the spectator now do? He fears that all may yet be lost, so he shouts to the Emperor to have courage, that the hunter is coming.

How does the author show his relief from the strain of the last few moments? His sentences are now longer and smoother.

How was this event afterwards regarded? The peasants maintained that an angel came down to their master's rescue.

What does the author seem to think? That his rescue was due to the interposition of Providence.

What is told in the next paragraph? Zyps' reward.

What did he receive? He was created a Count and received a pension from the Emperor.

What was his title? "Count Hallooer von Hohenfeldsen."

To what does this refer? To his "wild cry" from the high peaks, when he saw the Emperor in danger.

How can you prove that this story is true? By inspecting the pension list of the Royal House of Hapsburg and by looking at a cross in the mountains that has been erected on the very spot where Maximilian was rescued.

II

Whom do you see in the second vision? The Emperor Charles V. pursued by his enemies.

Who was he? One of the greatest monarchs in Europe, greater even than his grandfather, Maximilian I. In this scene he is ill; his army has met with reverses; he has made his escape from Innsbruck, the capital of the Tyrol, and is being conveyed through the mountains to a place of safety, closely pursued by Maurice of Saxony.

Describe the scene. It is at night, the wind is high, and is driving the rain against the Emperor's litter, which is borne by mountaineers and surrounded by his faithful officers.

What is given in the first paragraph? A description of the storm.

How does the author prepare you for the scene? The night suggests danger and mystery, and the moon looks out from a cloud, as though at something taking place in the gorge. The spectator hears something besides the roar of the wind.

Select all the words that show what a fearful night it is. "Night", "dark", "wild", "gusty winds", "howling", "sheets of blinding rain", "whirling", "hissing eddies", "rent asunder", "ravings of the tempest".

Notice all the details the author has made use of to convey the idea of terror and danger.

What is described in the next paragraph? The passage of the litter through the dark gorge.

Is the spectator forgotten in this scene? No, he first hears the "tramp of feet", then he sees the torches, and, lastly, the Emperor's litter surrounded by his attendants.

What words show you the difficulty of their situation? "Hurried", "crowding", "crushing", "steep and narrow gorge", "suppressed voices", "fitful glancing of torches", "anxiously shielded", "melée", "struggle onward".

Why are their voices suppressed? As a natural result of their perilous position.

Why do they keep their torches burning? To find their way through the enemy's country amid the dangers by which they are surrounded.

What do the lamps look like? A "constellation" of stars moving on in the same relative position.

Does the author still refer to the storm? Yes, in "derisive laughter", "rude wrath of the tempest", and "plumes streaming on the wind". The author wishes to picture continuously the fitting surroundings for this adventure, and so emphasizes these details.

Why does he speak of the "derisive laughter of the storm"? He compares it to a fiend who mocks the attempts of man to battle against his power.

Who is described in the third paragraph of this vision? The Emperor himself.

Why is he not described before, as he is more important than either the storm or his comrades? The story runs in a natural order. First are seen the figures surrounding the litter, and, as it approaches, the Emperor's face is distinguishable.

What is first mentioned in connection with him? His firmly set teeth.

What does this indicate? His great physical pain, and his determination of character.

What is mentioned next? His age; he is but fifty-three, but his wrinkles are deep and his hair turning gray.

What are next described? His forehead, his nose, his eye, his underlip.

Why does the author picture these features in such detail? To show the character of the Emperor.

What are we led to infer are some of his characteristics? A strong intellect, imperious manner, cruelty, and stubborn pride.

What strong contrast is drawn? The fugitive invalid is the great Emperor. The author first discusses his illness, his flight, his suffering in the storm, his adverse fortune, and then gives him his full titles—"Emperor of Germany, King of Spain, Lord of the Netherlands, of Naples, of Lombardy, and the proud chief of the golden Western World".

Where does the author place the blame for his present sufferings? On Charles himself, whose sufferings, humiliation, and ultimate deliverance were perhaps intended as a discipline to lead him to repent for past cruelties.

What is described in the last paragraph of this scene? The escape.

Who is first mentioned? The pursuer, Maurice of Saxony.

Describe him. He is first compared to an "avenger of blood" in pursuit of a man fleeing to the cities of refuge referred to in Joshua xx. 3. He is next compared to the hound relentlessly following his prey.

Who wins in this race? Charles eludes his pursuer.

To whom should he show gratitude for his escape? To Providence.

Does he acknowledge God's protection? No, he gives all the credit to his "lucky star".

Explain this. Astrologers had said that the "Star of Austria" was always at the highest point in the heavens; and of this favoured House of Austria, Charles was Archduke.

III

The first scene is called "The Rescue"; the second, "The Run"; and the last, "The Ruin". What is described in the last scene? The destruction of the French Army.

Where is the scene laid? In the Tyrol, beside the River Inn.

What is described in the first paragraph? Bonaparte's decree that the strongholds of his enemies—the Tyrolese warrior hunters—shall be destroyed.

Why should he wish to do this? The Tyrolese were an independent people, who would not submit to conscription and taxation at the hands of the Bavarians.

By what names does the author call Napoleon? "Bonaparte." That was his surname. The French Emperor had no hereditary right to the throne, but he wished to be called Napoleon, instead of Bonaparte, just as we speak of our King as George V. and rarely refer to his surname of Guelph.

Who advised Napoleon? "His own will is his sole adviser." He ruled arbitrarily, consulting no one.

What does he do in this case? He sends ten thousand French and Bavarian soldiers to crush the Tyrolese.

Why were the Bavarians taking part in the struggle? They were at this time allies of France, and Napoleon had given to their Elector possession of this new but hostile province.

What does the second paragraph describe? The army entering the narrow gorge in the mountains.

How does the author give vividness to this picture? He endows inanimate things such as the "gorge" and the "river" with human attributes. The "gorge" looks gloomy, forbidding, and unfriendly, and the "river" seems to roar indignantly, as though at the attempt of "the mountain walls" to impede its progress.

The next sentence is in the form of a question and its answer. Who is supposed to ask this question? This is the question the leader of the army would ask and the answer he would make when he discovered the narrow road. The construction of the sentence suggests the idea of danger.

Why does the next sentence begin with "But"? "But the glittering array winds on." It suggests that some precautions for the safety of the army should have been observed; but it may have been impossible to take these precautions, and the orders of Bonaparte had to be obeyed at all hazards.

What is described in the next sentence? The author gives full details of the progress of this imposing army. The River Inn seems to share the feelings of the Tyrolese themselves and protest angrily against this invasion by a foreign power.

How is the next sentence related to the preceding? "But" marks a contrast. The noise of the army and the river is contrasted with the silence on the heights.

Why are the "eagles" mentioned? The silence is rendered more impressive by the occasional "shrill cry" of the eagles, and the "wings" of the eagles hovering above are an omen of the coming disaster which is to overtake "the gilded eagles of France" below.

What is described in the next paragraph? The "voice" from the "heights".

How does the author make this paragraph impressive? As he wishes to indicate the critical moment, he still uses the present tense, direct narration, short sentences, exclamation, and interrogation; he suggests, through a mysterious voice far up the heights, that supernatural agents are at work. The army, in its helpless length, is compared to an "uncoiled serpent".

What is the subject of the next paragraph? The destruction of the entire army.

How is this ruin accomplished? Unseen in the heights above, the Tyrolese peasantry hurl down rocks, roots, and trunks of pine trees, as well as sending a "deadly hail" from their rifles along the "whole line" of the defenceless army below.

Notice the richness of detail. What words help to make the description of their destruction more vivid? "Bounding", "thundering", "gathering speed", "headlong way", "launched down", "powerless foe", "deadly hail", "fearful storm", "crushed to death", "tumbled, horse and man, into the choked and swollen river".

Notice the contrast of this paragraph with the picture in the second paragraph of this vision of the gallant invading army.

What is the subject of the last paragraph? The reflections of the author.

Of what does he speak? Of the wonders and beauties of creation and the sad power that man possesses of spoiling and staining these wonders by giving rein to his own "evil ambitions and fierce revenges".

How has he emphasized this? By the use of exclamation, question, ellipses, and the mention of the "serpent" as the symbol of evil.

How does the interrogative form of the sentence give it vividness? Contrast the effect of saying, "Who would willingly linger on the hideous details?" with "No one would willingly linger", etc. The author does not expect an answer, he throws the sentence into the question form for the rhetorical effect. The reader pays more attention to the thought by trying to find an answer to the question.

What is the value of the ellipses in "Sorrowful that man ... should come"? It is stronger than saying, "It is sorrowful that man ... should come". The subject and verb are omitted, as they are not strong words, and "Sorrowful" is placed in the most prominent position on account of its importance.

SUMMARY

In these three pictures, what is the constant element? The scene used as the background. All three visions take place in the Tyrol, two of them on the banks of the Inn River. They are three companion pictures of this historic mountain province.

How does this style compare with that which you find in other lessons? It is abrupt and abounds in many rhetorical forms—

ellipses, use of the present tense, exclamation, direct address, and accumulation of details.

Would it be suitable for all prose expression? No; it is impassioned prose, full of emotion and picturesque detail. The smoother, more regulated sentence-structure, such as is in place in ordinary narration, would be too cold for these descriptions. On the other hand, this style is not suitable for expressing a quiet mood or giving a clear explanation. It is too turbulent, and would pall upon the reader if continued at too great length, but it is often very suitable in an oratorical selection.

The pupils should finally read the lesson aloud, to show how they have appreciated the story.

CHAPTER VIII

SUPPLEMENTARY READING

Before studying these lessons in supplementary reading, it is suggested that the teacher read again what has been said on "Extensive Reading", p. 39 of this Manual.

SOUTH-WEST WIND, ESQ.

(Third Reader, page 86)

You have read the story of South-West Wind, Esq., in the Third Reader.

Who were the persons mentioned in this story? Three brothers, Schwartz, Hans, and Gluck.

What were their characters? Schwartz and Hans were rich but very miserly; they were quarrelsome, drunken, and cruel. Gluck was kind, polite, and unselfish.

How did Gluck show these qualities? He admitted the stranger into the house for shelter from the rain, when he knew his brothers would punish him for so doing; he asked politely to take the stranger's cloak, when the water dripping from it was putting the fire out; and he offered him his share of the mutton, although he knew it meant that he must go without his own supper.

When the older brothers returned what did they do? They tried to punish Gluck and to force the stranger out of the house.

What happened? They were hurled to the ground by the stranger, who was much stronger than they supposed.

What other punishment did they receive? The roof was blown off the house while they slept, and their beautiful valley, together with their crops and cattle, was utterly destroyed by the heavy rains.

Who was the stranger? He left his card with "South-West Wind, Esq." written on it.

Now the story in the Reader is only the first chapter of a longer story, which relates what fortune came to the three brothers.

What should you expect would happen to them? I should expect that Schwartz and Hans would have more troubles, and that Gluck would be rewarded for his kind-heartedness.

CHAPTER II

Read the second chapter of this longer story called *The King of the Golden River*.

Give me the main points in this chapter?

1. The valley was turned into a desert.
2. The brothers became goldsmiths.
3. The mug
4. Gluck's wish that the river would turn into gold
5. The voice from the furnace
6. The dwarf
7. The King told Gluck how the river could be turned into gold.

What are the characters of the two brothers in this chapter? They were very dishonest and even tried to mix copper with the gold. They were drunken and wasted their money, and they were lazy and cruel.

Describe the mug that was being melted. It had been given to them by their uncle, and Gluck was very fond of it. It was made of gold almost in the form of a human face. The face was fierce and red, the eyes were bright, the beard and whiskers were of fine gold, and the hair was of fine spun gold, forming the handle of the mug.

While the mug was being melted in the furnace, what did Gluck see as he looked out of the window? The range of mountains overhanging Treasure Valley, with the mountain tops shining in the sunset.

This is a lovely description of a sunset in the mountains. Pick out the details of the picture. "Rocks ... all crimson and purple with the sunset", "bright tongues of fiery cloud", "the river ... a waving column of pure gold", "the double arch of a broad purple rainbow", "flushing and fading alternately in the wreaths of spray".

What words suggest colours? "Crimson", "purple", "fiery", "pure gold", "purple rainbow", "flushing", "fading".

What did this picture suggest to Gluck? It made him wish that the river were really gold.

Describe the dwarf who came out of the furnace. He was a foot and a half high; his hair and beard were long, curled, and delicate, and his face was copper-coloured.

Account for the dwarf being in such a place. It was owing to the malicious enchantment of a king stronger than himself that he had been turned into the golden mug, and, when the mug was melted, Gluck poured out the metal, and, thus freed the King of the Golden River from the power of his enemy.

How did the King show his gratitude? He told Gluck how the river could be turned into gold.

What must Gluck do in order to gain this end? He must climb to the top of the mountain and cast three drops of holy water into the stream at its source.

CHAPTER III

What are the main facts in this chapter?

1. The brothers returned and beat Gluck because the mug was a total loss.
2. Schwartz and Hans fought.
3. Schwartz was arrested.
4. Hans stole a cupful of holy water.
5. Hans taunted Schwartz.
6. Hans attempted to change the river to gold. (1) The dog; (2) the fair child; (3) the old man.
7. Hans was changed into the Black Stone.

What characteristics of the older brothers are shown in this chapter? They were drunken, brutal, quarrelsome, dishonest, malicious, and selfish.

Why are the dog, the child, and the old man introduced into the story? To show how indifferent Hans was to the suffering of animals, children, and aged people. The sight of these helpless creatures should have aroused his pity.

Were there any indications in the story that Hans would be unsuccessful? Yes, there was "a strange shadow"; the air "seemed to throw his blood into a fever"; "a dark gray cloud came over the sun"; "long, snake-like shadows"; "leaden weight of the dead air"; "flash of blue lightning"; "tongues of fire"; "flashes of bloody light".

Why was Hans unsuccessful? He had led a bad life, had been dishonest, and had been selfish to the dog, the child, and the aged man.

Show that it was an appropriate punishment that Hans should be turned into a Black Stone. His heart was as hard as stone, and his deeds were black.

CHAPTER IV

What is the main theme of this chapter? Schwartz's attempt to turn the river into gold.

What are the chief incidents recorded?

1. Gluck paid Schwartz's fine.
2. Schwartz refused water to the child, the old man, and to the spirit of Hans.
3. He was also changed to a Black Stone.

What were the indications that Schwartz would be unsuccessful? There was a "black cloud rising out of the West"; "a mist of the colour of blood"; "waves of the angry sea"; "bursts of spiry lightning"; "the sky was like ... a lake of blood"; "its waves were black, like thunderclouds"; "their foam was like fire"; "the lightning glared into his eyes".

CHAPTER V

What is the theme in the last chapter? Gluck's attempt to turn the river into gold.

Give the main incidents.

1. The priest gave him holy water.
2. He gave water to the aged man and the child.
3. He gave his last drop of water to the dying dog.
4. The dog was transformed into the King of the Golden River.
5. He gave Gluck three drops of dew.
6. Gluck cast the water into the river.
7. Treasure Valley again became a fertile garden, and Gluck became very rich.

What were the indications that Gluck would be successful? After giving the old man some water, the "path became easier"; "grasshoppers began singing"; there was "bright green moss"; "pale pink starry flowers"; "soft belled gentians"; "pure white transparent lilies"; "its waves were as clear as crystal".

What strong contrast is brought out in this story? There is a contrast between this chapter and the two preceding ones. Gluck's conduct is so different from that of Schwartz and Hans; and the aspect of nature, as it appears to him, is very different from the scenes viewed by his brothers.

Describe Treasure Valley after it was changed. The "fresh grass sprang beside the new streams"; "creeping plants grew"; "young flowers opened"; "thickets of myrtle and tendrils of vine cast lengthening shadows"; "his barns became full of corn and his house of treasure".

Why did Gluck deserve so much kindness? He had been hospitable to South-West Wind, Esq.; had suffered hunger and punishment on his account; had been industrious; had freed the King of the Golden River from his enchantment; had obeyed his instructions; had felt sorry for Hans; had paid Schwartz's fine; and had shown mercy to animals and helpless people.

Was there anything said about the two older brothers? Yes, there are two black stones, which people still call "The Black Brothers", at the top of the cataract. This story tells how these stones came to be there.

A CHRISTMAS CAROL

(Fourth Reader, page 39)

The pupils have read *Scrooge's Christmas,* in the Fourth Reader. They have also read the synopsis of *A Christmas Carol* at the beginning of the lesson. If they have read the first four *staves* of the carol in a general way, they will be in a better position to study intensively the last stave, or chapter, which is the lesson in the Reader. They will understand the causes that have changed this "covetous old sinner" to the man "who knew how to keep Christmas Day well". This lesson should be taken up near Christmas. The pupils will discuss Stave I, after having read it at home.

Stave I

What is the title of this work? A Christmas Carol.

Why is it called a carol? In England, it is the custom for bands of singers, called "waits", to go from house to house on Christmas Eve. The author calls this ghost story of Christmas a carol in prose, for it pictures the joys and sorrows of this season.

What does a stave mean? It keeps up the idea of a carol. Each chapter is called a stave, or stanza of the carol.

What is the title of the first stave? "Marley's Ghost."

Who was Marley? He had been Scrooge's partner, but was now dead. He had been as miserly as Scrooge himself.

Where is the scene laid? In London.

When? On Christmas Eve.

Describe Scrooge. "Oh but he was a tight-fisted hand ... one degree at Christmas". (See Stave I of *A Christmas Carol.*)

Notice the wonderful accumulation of strong adjectives and phrases in this description. Why does the author use so many? He wishes to emphasize the cold miserliness of this man.

What is the first incident? Scrooge's treatment of his nephew, who has invited him to dinner on Christmas Day.

What does this incident show? His churlishness, and his contempt for those who spend money freely.

What is the next incident? His refusal to subscribe to any charities in the city.

What comes next? The account of his treatment of Bob Cratchit.

What does this show? His meanness and tyranny.

When he returns from his supper, what does he encounter? Marley's Ghost.

What does the ghost tell him? How it must wander through the world without rest, in atonement for Marley's cruelties and his neglect of other people. It laments his misspent life.

What does it promise to do to Scrooge? It promises to send him "Three Spirits".

What good description is found in Stave I? Besides the character sketch of Scrooge, there is a picture of Christmas Eve in the London streets, in the paragraph beginning "Meanwhile the fog and darkness thickened".

Stave II

What is described in this chapter? The visit of the first spirit.

What was it? The "Ghost of Christmas Past".

Read me a description of it. "It was a strange figure ... like a child ... which it held under its arm".

What does the spirit do? It forces Scrooge to accompany it and shows him former Christmas scenes in his life.

What are these scenes? Scrooge as a solitary boy at school; his boyhood stories, *Ali Baba* and *Robinson Crusoe;* his sister; Fezziwig's ball; Scrooge's sweetheart; scenes in her married life.

What is the mood of these different scenes? There is humour, and a great deal of fun, as well as some pathos. It is all told in a lively style.

What are the best descriptions? Fezziwig's ball, and the remembrance of the scenes in *Ali Baba*.

Stave III

What is told in this chapter? The visit of the second spirit.

Who was it? The "Spirit of Christmas Present".

What does it show Scrooge? Scenes of Christmas shopping; Christmas out-of-doors; the Grocers; Bob Cratchit's family, the goose, their dinner, the puddings; the miner's home; the lighthouse keepers; the sailors; Scrooge's nephew at home—blindman's bluff, forfeits, Yes and No; vision of "Ignorance" and "Want".

What do all these scenes go to show? How different kinds of people keep Christmas; how kind and merry most people are at this season of the year: and how some have to struggle in order to get this one day's pleasure.

Select some examples of humour. Peter's conceit, some of the descriptions of the grocery stores, the anticipations lest harm befall the goose and the pudding.

Select any examples of pathos. The references to Tiny Tim.

Select and read the best descriptions. The grocery stores, the fruit stores, the goose, the pudding.

Stave IV

What is told in this chapter? The visit of the third spirit.

What was it? The "Ghost of Christmas Yet to Come".

What does it show Scrooge? A vision of his death—how he is plundered by laundress, charwoman, and undertaker; the phantom of Death; Scrooge's creditors; the grave.

Had these scenes actually taken place? No, but they will be realized if Scrooge does not change his manner of thinking and living.

What is the effect of these three visions? Scrooge promises the "Ghost of Christmas Yet to Come" "I will honour Christmas in my heart and try to keep it all the year".

Why are the scenes in this chapter not so pleasant as those that the two former spirits had shown him? The scenes that the first spirit had brought before him were his joys at the Christmas season before he had hardened his heart; those that the second spirit had shown were scenes in the lives of people who do something for others and enjoy themselves in the true Christmas spirit; those that the last spirit had shown were the sordid scenes which would be sure to come if he did not change his attitude toward life. The last scenes shown him by the third spirit furnish a strong contrast to the others.

Stave V

What does this chapter relate? How Scrooge actually kept Christmas Day.

What were the other chapters about? The first and the last were the only chapters where he was awake. Chapters Two, Three, and Four are visions or dreams. Notice how the phantom changed into the bed-post.

This chapter should be studied closely. Who wrote this story? Charles Dickens, an English novelist.

Do you know any other good stories by the same author? *David Copperfield, The Pickwick Papers, Nicholas Nickleby.*

Yes, we have had extracts in the Readers from these books.

What lessons are they? *The Pickwick Club on the Ice,* in the *Third Book; David Copperfield's First Journey Alone,* and *The Indignation of Nicholas Nickleby* in the *Fourth Book.*

Some day you must read these stories. *David Copperfield* tells us a great deal about Dickens' early days. *The Pickwick Papers* is full of humour in scenes such as that depicted in *The Pickwick Club on the Ice,* and has some fine characters in it, and *Nicholas Nickleby* gives a vivid picture of the brutality existing in some schools in England at the time the book was written.

THE LADY OF THE LAKE

(Fourth Reader, page 270)

The pupils will have read the account of the stirring combat between Fitz-James and Roderick Dhu. They will be curious to know the circumstances that led up to this combat and also the conclusion of the story.

The aim of the teacher is to lead the pupils to appreciate the construction of the story, the fine character sketches, and the descriptions of natural scenery, as well as to give them an impression of Highland life. The pupils will take delight in the rapid movement of the verse and in the deeds of valour.

Some passages should be dwelt upon at greater length by the teacher, and others more lightly touched upon, so that the connections of the various parts will be understood. A close and tedious consideration of all the lines would not show a good critical taste, as some passages are very fine, while others have only ordinary merit.

The teacher should disclose the identity of Fitz-James as James V of Scotland

and should explain the cause of the exile of the Douglas Family. He should also sketch the life of rebellion and consequent outlawry led by some of the Highland clans before they were reduced to submission.

CANTO I

The teacher should study with the pupils the Invocation of the three opening stanzas and ask them to read the first canto. He should next discuss it briefly, as suggested in the following outline:

What are the main divisions of the first canto?

1. The chase
2. Description of the Trossachs
3. Description of Ellen Douglas
4. Description of Fitz-James.

Why is the story of the chase introduced? It brings Fitz-James alone into the enemy's country, where he meets Ellen Douglas, and prepares the way for the adventures that follow.

What is the story of the chase? The hundred huntsmen and the horses and the dogs become wearied in the long pursuit after the stag. One huntsman alone is left to enter the deep ravine where the stag escapes.

This description of the Trossachs made the spot famous, and ever since it has been a favourite resort of tourists.

CANTO II

The Island

What are the divisions of this canto?

1. The departure of the huntsmen
2. Description of the minstrel
3. The story of Roderick's love
4. Return of the Clan-Alpine
5. Malcolm Graeme
6. The quarrel.

What is the value of this canto? It explains many facts that we did not understand. Among others, it shows us the relation of the Douglases to the King and to Roderick Dhu. It tells of the love of Malcolm Graeme for Ellen and of Roderick's hopeless love for her. It shows us Roderick's noble traits of character and the fearful cruelties of which he is capable. He cannot possibly win Ellen's love.

CANTO III

The Gathering

What are the main divisions of this canto?

1. Roderick's determination to renew hostilities
2. Brian the Hermit
3. The ceremony
4. The message of the Fiery Cross
5. Roderick's devotion to Ellen
6. The gathering.

What are the best passages in this canto?

1. Description of Loch Katrine
2. The coronach
3. Hymn to the Virgin.

Why are funeral and wedding scenes introduced? These serve to show how the message of the Fiery Cross was looked upon as more important than even death or marriage.

What insight into the life of the clansmen is furnished in this canto?

1 The superstition of the Highlanders. This is shown in Brian's faith and in the weird ceremonies in connection with the Fiery Cross.

2. The method of mustering the clans by means of the message of the Fiery Cross.

3. Their funerals and weddings.

Notice also the vigour of the stanzas that describe the flight of Malise.

CANTO IV

The Prophecy

Give the main themes in this canto.

1. Return of Malise
2. Norman's guard
3. The augury and the prophecy
4. Return of Fitz-James to Ellen Douglas
5. The ring
6. Blanche of Devan
7. Death of Murdoch

8. Fitz-James meets Roderick Dhu.

What are the best stanzas? The ballad of "Alice Brand".

Why is this ballad introduced? It shows the character of Scottish minstrelsy, the belief in the world of fairies, and the lesson of hope that at the darkest moment the hour of happiness may be near. It furnishes another example of Allanbane's prophetic insight.

The introduction: "The rose is fairest when it is budding new." Why is this stanza appropriate? It shows the tenderness of Norman's love, as contrasted with the fierce warfare in which he is engaged.

Why is Blanche of Devan introduced? To furnish an example of Roderick's cruelty, so that Fitz-James should feel justified in punishing him. Blanche of Devan also warns Fitz-James of Murdoch's treachery. This stanza explains the allusions in the lesson in the *Fourth Book*, for example: "a braid of your fair lady's hair", and "There lies red Murdoch stark and stiff".

What characteristics of Roderick are shown in the canto?

1. His care for the defenceless in his clan
2. His cruelty to his enemies
3. His hospitality
4. His superstition.

What was the prophecy?

Who spills the foremost foeman's life
That party conquers in the strife.

What is the value of the prophecy in the poem? It furnishes a reason for the eagerness of the clansmen to take the life of the huntsman, as the former would then "conquer in the strife".

CANTO V

The Combat

Give the main events in this canto.

1. Roderick guides Fitz-James to neutral ground
2. The combat
3. Douglas surrenders
4. The games
5. The popularity of Douglas.

What is the most striking part of this canto? The story of the combat.

Why? It is a fine example of Scottish bravery and chivalry.

What Scottish characteristics are found in this canto?

1. The character of Scottish games in the city
2. The fickleness of the mob
3. The chivalrous conduct of the combatants.

CANTO VI

The Guard-room

What are the main themes in this canto?

1. The rough soldiers
2. Ellen presents the ring
3. The battle of Beal' an Duine
4. Death of Roderick
5. Ellen's request to James
6. Happiness of the Douglases and of Malcolm Graeme
7. Farewell to the Harp.

Why are the rough soldiers introduced? This passage furnishes a good description of the character of the soldiers, and shows the power of Ellen's quiet dignity and modesty.

What is the value of the battle of Beal' an Duine? It affords an opportunity to the valiant Roderick to imagine himself in battle, so that when death comes he does not realize that it finds him a prisoner and his clan vanquished.

How does the poem end? Ellen, her father, and Malcolm Graeme are united and happy, and Fitz-James reveals his identity and shows his magnanimity.

What should be read in connection with the last three stanzas? The first three stanzas of the poem. They are an Invocation to Scottish minstrelsy. We now have the Farewell.

Which cantos do you consider are the best? The first and the fifth.

Why? The first contains such wonderful word-pictures and the fifth seems to be the crisis of the story. The interest is not sustained in the sixth canto, as one knows matters are sure to be adjusted.

CHAPTER IX

SELECTIONS FOR MEMORIZATION

Little deeds of kindness,
Little words of love,
Make our earth an Eden,
Like the heaven above.—BREWER

God make my life a little light,
Within the world to glow,—
A little flame that burneth bright.
Wherever I may go.

The world is so full of a number of things,
I'm sure we should all be as happy as kings.—STEVENSON

Be kind and be gentle
To those who are old,
For dearer is kindness
And better than gold.

Politeness is to *do* and *say*
The kindest thing in the kindest way.

Two ears and only one mouth have you;
The reason, I think, is clear:
It teaches, my child, that it will not do
To talk about all you hear.

Whene'er a task is set for you,
Don't idly sit and view it,
Nor be content to wish it done;
Begin at once and do it.

Work while you work, play while you play;
This is the way to be cheerful and gay.
All that you do, do with your might;
Things done by halves are never done right.—STODART

Five things observe with care,—
Of whom you speak, to whom you speak
And how, and when, and where.—GRAY

See that little sunbeam
Darting through the room,
Scattering the darkness,
Lighting up the gloom.
Let me be a sunbeam
Everywhere I go,
Making glad and happy
Every one I know.

Sing a song of seasons!
Something bright in all!
Flowers in the summer,
Fires in the fall!—STEVENSON

Do all the good you can,
In all the ways you can,
To all the people you can,
Just as long as you can.

When you come to think of it,
The day is what you make it;
And whether good, or whether bad,
Depends on how you take it.

Slumber, slumber, little one, now
The bird is asleep in his nest on the bough;
The bird is asleep, he has folded his wings,
And over him softly the dream fairy sings:

> Lullaby, lullaby—lullaby!
> Pearls in the deep—
> Stars in the sky,
> Dreams in our sleep;
> So lullaby!—F. D. SHERMAN

Dare to be true; nothing can need a lie.

The face you wear, the thoughts you bring,
A heart may heal or break.

He who is good at making excuses is seldom good for anything else.—FRANKLIN

To *be* good is the mother of to *do* good.

I'll not willingly offend,
Nor be easily offended;
What's amiss I'll try to mend,
And endure what can't be mended.

A man of words and not of deeds,
Is like a garden full of weeds;
For when the weeds begin to grow,
Then doth the garden overflow.

Little children, you must seek
Rather to be good than wise,
For the thoughts you do not speak
Shine out in your cheeks and eyes.—ALICE CARY

To tell a falsehood is like the cut of a sabre; for though the wound may heal, the scar of it will remain.—SADI

All that's great and good is done
Just by patient trying.

'Tis a lesson you should heed,
Try, try again;
If at first you don't succeed,
Try, try again.

If a task is once begun,
Never leave it till it's done;
Be the labour great or small,
Do it well, or not at all.

For every evil under the sun,
There is a remedy, or there is none.
If there be one, try to find it;
If there be none, never mind it.

There are many flags in many lands,
There are flags of every hue,
But there is no flag in any land
Like our own Red, White, and Blue.

The inner side of every cloud
Is always bright and shining;
And so I turn my clouds about,
And always wear them inside out,
To show the silver lining.

I would not hurt a living thing,
However weak or small;
The beasts that graze, the birds that sing,
Our Father made them all.

Little drop of dew,
Like a gem you are;
I believe that you
Must have been a star.
When the day is bright,
On the grass you lie;
Tell me then, at night
Are you in the sky?—F. D. Sherman

How beautiful is the rain!
After the dust and the heat,
In the broad and fiery street,
In the narrow lane,
How beautiful is the rain!—Longfellow

In spring, when stirs the wind, I know
That soon the crocus buds will show;
For 'tis the wind who bids them wake
And into pretty blossoms break.—F. D. Sherman

O, pause and think for a moment
What a desolate land it would be,
If, east or west, the eye should rest
On not a single tree! —GRAY

It was only a sunny smile,
And little it cost in the giving,
But it scattered the night,
Like the morning light,
And made the day worth living.

Keep pushing—'tis wiser
Than sitting aside,
And dreaming and sighing,
And waiting the tide.
In life's earnest battle,
They only prevail
Who daily march onward,
And never say "fail".

One step and then another,
And the longest walk is ended.
One stitch and then another,
And the largest rent is mended.
One brick and then another,
And the highest wall is made.
One flake and then another,
And the deepest snow is laid.

Speak the truth and speak it ever,
Cost it what it will.
He who hides the wrong he did,
Does the wrong thing still.

Whichever way the wind doth blow,
Some heart is glad to have it so;
Then blow it east or blow it west,
The wind that blows, that wind is best.

We should make the same use of books that the bee does of a flower: he gathers sweets from it, but does not injure it.

I smile, and then the Sun comes out;
He hides away whene'er I pout;
He seems a very funny sun,
To do whatever he sees done.
And when it rains he disappears;
Like me, he can't see through the tears.
Now isn't that the reason why
I ought to smile and never cry?—F. D. SHERMAN

If fortune, with a smiling face,
Strew roses in our way,
When shall we stoop to pick them up?
To-day, my friend, to-day.
If those who've wronged us own their faults,
And kindly pity pray,
When shall we listen and forgive?
To-day, my friend, to-day.

Are you almost disgusted with life, little man?
I will tell you a wonderful trick
That will bring you contentment if anything can—
Do something for somebody, quick.
Are you very much tired with play, little girl?
Weary, discouraged, and sick?
I'll tell you the loveliest game in the world—
Do something for somebody, quick.

"Were it not for me",
Said a chickadee,
"Not a single flower on earth would be;
For under the ground they soundly sleep,
And never venture an upward peep,
Till they hear from me,
Chickadee-dee-dee!" —SIDNEY DAYRE

The world at noon belongs to the sun,
At eve to the home-coming herds;
But while the dew is early—very, very early—
The world belongs to the birds.
As still as in a dream lie the meadows and the stream,
'Neath the soaring and outpouring of the birds.—WETHERALD

I know, blue modest violets,
Gleaming with dew at morn—
I know the place you come from,
And the way that you are born!
When God cuts holes in Heaven,
The holes the stars look through,
He lets the scraps fall down to earth,—
The little scraps are you.

The blossoms, down in the meadow,
In the gardens, and woods, and the hills,
Are singing, too, with their playmates,
The birds, and the breezes, and rills.
And I think, if you listen closely,
In the sweet glad days of spring,
With the song of the brook, the breeze, and the birds,
You can hear the flowers sing.—MOOREHOUSE

Good-night, little shivering grasses!
'Tis idle to struggle and fight
With tempest and cruel frost-fingers;
Lie down, little grasses, to-night!
Good-night, little shivering grasses!
Lie down 'neath the coverlet white,
And rest till the cuckoo is singing;
Good-night, little grasses, good-night!—*A November Good-night.*—BEERS

Daffydowndilly came up in the cold,
Through the brown mould,
Although the March breezes blew keen on her face,
Although the white snow lay on many a place.
I can't do much yet, but I'll do what I can.
It's well I began!
For unless I can manage to lift up my head,
The people will think that the Spring herself's dead.
O Daffydowndilly, so brave and so true,
I wish all were like you!
So ready for duty in all sorts of weather,
And holding forth courage and beauty together.—WARNER

One to-day is worth two to-morrow's.—POOR RICHARD'S ALMANAC

The future is purchased by the present.—SAMUEL JOHNSON

The sober second thought is always essential, and seldom wrong.—MARTIN VAN BUREN

Recollect that trifles make perfection, and that perfection is no trifle.—MICHAEL ANGELO

Have more than thou showest,
Speak less than thou knowest.—SHAKESPEARE

Sin has many tools, but a lie is the handle that fits them all.—O. W. HOLMES

Let all the end thou aim'st at be thy country's,
Thy God's and truth's.—SHAKESPEARE

Our greatest glory is not in never falling, but in rising every time we fall.

Learn to obey and you will know how to command.—LUBBOCK

One who is contented with what he has done will never become famous for what he will do.

Be not simply good, be good for something.—THOREAU

The better part of valour is discretion.—SHAKESPEARE

They that touch pitch will be defiled.—SHAKESPEARE

Ill blows the wind that profits nobody.—SHAKESPEARE

Honour and shame from no condition rise;
Act well your part, there all the honour lies.—POPE

True happiness consists not in the multitude of friends, but in their worth and choice.—BEN JONSON

One "do" is worth a thousand "don'ts" in the destruction of evil or the production of good.—HUGHES

I look upon the simple and childish virtues of veracity and honesty as the root of all that is sublime in character.—EMERSON

Remember that though it is a good thing to be a great man, it is a great thing to be a good man.

Striving not to be rich or great,
Never questioning fortune or fate,
Contented slowly to earn, and wait.

In the workshop, on the farm,
Or wherever you may be,
From your future efforts, boys,
Comes a nation's destiny.

It is a low benefit to give me something; it is a high benefit to enable me to do something of myself.—EMERSON

Greatly begin! though thou hast time
But for a line, be that sublime,—
Not failure, but low aim, is crime.—LOWELL

Never give up! 'Tis the secret of glory;
Nothing so wise can philosophy preach;
Look at the lives that are famous in story;
"Never give up" is the lesson they teach.

It is a good thing to be rich, and a good thing to be strong, but it is a better thing to be beloved of many friends.—EURIPIDES

Do what conscience says is right;
Do what reason says is best;
Do with all your mind and might;
Do your duty, and be blest.

What men want is not talent, it is purpose; in other words, not the power to achieve, but the will to labour.—BULWER-LYTTON

So nigh is grandeur to our dust,
So near is God to man,
When Duty whispers low, *Thou must,*
The soul replies *I can.*—EMERSON

Habit is a cable; we weave a thread of it each day, and it becomes so strong we cannot break it.—HORACE MANN

Ponder well, and know the right,
Onward then, with all thy might!
Haste not! years can ne'er atone
For one reckless action done.—GOETHE

Our grand business is not to see what lies dimly at a distance, but to do what lies clearly at hand.—CARLYLE

Slight is the stin3g of his trouble whose winnings are less than
his worth:
For he who is honest is noble, whatever his fortune or
birth.—ALICE CARY

Press on! There's no such word as fail!
Push nobly on! The goal is near!
Ascend the mountain! Breast the gale!
Look upward, onward—never fear!

He who has a thousand friends
Has not a friend to spare;
And he who has one enemy
Will meet him everywhere.—OMAR KHAYYAM

Work for some good, be it ever so slowly;
Cherish some flower, be it ever so lowly;
Labour!—all labour is noble and holy.—FRANCES S. OSGOOD

A man should never be ashamed to own he has been in the wrong; which is but saying in other words that he is wiser to-day than he was yesterday.—POPE

Tender-handed stroke a nettle,
And it stings you for your pains;
Grasp it like a man of mettle,
And it soft as silk remains.

Fill up each hour with what will last;
Buy up the moments as they go;
The life above, when this is past,
Is the ripe fruit of life below.

New occasions teach new duties; time makes ancient
good uncouth;
They must upward still and onward, who would keep abreast of
Truth.—LOWELL

The heights by great men reached and kept,
Were not attained by sudden flight;
But they, while their companions slept,
Were toiling upward in the night.—LONGFELLOW

Nothing useless is, or low,
Each thing in its place is best,
And what seems but idle show
Strengthens and supports the rest.—LONGFELLOW

And not by eastern windows only,
When daylight comes, comes in the light,
In front, the sun climbs slow, how slowly,
But westward, look, the land is bright.—CLOUGH

Full many a gem of purest ray serene
The dark unfathom'd caves of ocean bear;
Full many a flower is born to blush unseen,
And waste its sweetness on the desert air.—GRAY

If a man empties his purse into his head, no man can take it away from him. An investment in knowledge always pays the best interest.—BENJAMIN FRANKLIN

I do not know
Where falls the seed that I have tried to sow
With greatest care;
But I shall know

The meaning of each waiting hour below
Sometime, somewhere!

Lives of great men all remind us
We can make our lives sublime,
And, departing, leave behind us
Footprints on the sands of time;
Let us, then, be up and doing,
With a heart for any fate;
Still achieving, still pursuing,
Learn to labour and to wait.—LONGFELLOW

Begin while life is bright and young,
Work out each noble plan;
True knowledge lends a charm to youth,
And dignifies the man.
Then upward, onward, step by step,
With perseverance rise,
And emulate, with hearts of hope,
The good, the great, the wise.

The night has a thousand eyes,
And the day but one;
Yet the light of the bright world dies,
With the dying sun.
The mind has a thousand eyes,
And the heart but one;
Yet the light of a whole life dies
When love is done.—FRANCIS BOURDILLON

In the darkness as in daylight,
On the water as on land,
God's eye is looking on us,
And beneath us is His hand!
Death will find us soon or later,
On the deck or in the cot;
And we cannot meet him better
Than in working out our lot.—WHITTIER

The Royal Navy of England hath ever been its greatest defence and ornament; it is its ancient and natural strength—the floating bulwark of our Island.—BLACKSTONE'S *Commentaries*

It is the land that freemen till,
That sober-suited Freedom chose.
The land, where girt with friends or foes
A man may speak the thing he will;
A land of settled government,
A land of just and old renown,
Where Freedom slowly broadens down
From precedent to precedent.—TENNYSON

O triune kingdom of the brave,
O sea-girt island of the free,
O empire of the land and wave
Our hearts, our hands, are all for thee.
Stand, Canadians, firmly stand,
Round the flag of our Fatherland.—LACLEDE

Sharers of our glorious past,
Brothers, must we part at last?
Shall we not thro' good and ill
Cleave to one another still?
Britain's myriad voices call,
"Sons, be welded each and all
Into one Imperial whole,
One with Britain, heart and soul!
One life, one flag, one fleet, one Throne!"
Britons, hold your own!—TENNYSON

"England! What thou wert, thou art!"
Gird thee with thine ancient might.
Forth! and God defend the Right.—NEWBOLT

Believe not each accusing tongue,
As most weak people do;
But still believe that story wrong
Which ought not to be true.—SHERIDAN

He prayeth best who loveth best
All things, both great and small,
For the dear God who loveth us,
He made and loveth all.—COLERIDGE

For whatever men say in blindness,
And spite of the fancies of youth,
There's nothing so kingly as Kindness,
And nothing so royal as Truth.—ALICE CARY

To do something, however small, to make others happier and better, is the highest ambition, the most elevating hope, which can inspire a human being.—LUBBOCK

Small service is true service while it lasts.
Of humblest friends, bright creature! scorn not one:
The daisy, by the shadow that it casts,
Protects the lingering dew-drops from the sun.—WORDSWORTH

Look up and not down;
Look forward and not back;
Look out and not in;
And lend a hand.—HALE

Have you had a kindness shown?
Pass it on.
'Twas not given for you alone,
Pass it on.
Let it travel down the years,
Let it wipe another's tears;
Till in heaven the deed appears.
Pass it on.

A little spring had lost its way
Amid the grass and fern;
A passing stranger scooped a well
Where weary men might turn.
He walled it in, and hung with care,
A ladle on the brink;
He thought not of the deed he did,
But judged that Toil might drink.
He passed again; and lo! the well,
By summer never dried,
Had cooled ten thousand parchèd tongues,
And saved a life beside.—MACKAY

Evil is wrought by want of thought
As well as want of heart.—HOOD

Nature has given to men one tongue, but two ears, that we may hear from others twice as much as we speak.—EPICTETUS

Count that day lost whose low-descending sun
Views from thy hand no worthy action done.

If happiness have not her seat
And centre in the breast,
We may be wise or rich or great,
But never can be blest.—BURNS

A kindly act is a kernel sown,
That will grow to a goodly tree,
Shedding its fruit when time has flown,
Down the gulf of eternity.

If I can stop one heart from breaking,
I shall not live in vain;
If I can ease one life the aching,
Or cool one pain,
Or help one fainting robin
Into his nest again,
I shall not live in vain.—DICKINSON

It is pleasant to think, just under the snow,
That stretches so bleak and blank and cold,
Are beauty and warmth that we cannot know,
Green fields and leaves and blossoms of gold.

Under the green hedges after the snow,
There do the dear little violets grow,
Hiding their modest and beautiful heads
Under the hawthorn in soft, mossy beds.
Sweet as the roses, and blue as the sky,
Down there do the dear little violets lie;
Hiding their heads where they scarce may be seen,
By the leaves you may know where the violets have been.—MOULTRIE

The linnet is singing the wild wood through;
The fawn's bounding footsteps skim over the dew.
The butterfly flits round the blossoming tree,
And the cowslip and bluebell are bent by the bee;

All the creatures that dwell in the forest are gay,
And why should not I be as merry as they? — MITFORD

Do the duty which lies nearest thee!
Thy second duty will already have become clearer. — CARLYLE

Live truly, and thy life shall be
A great and noble creed.

I slept, and dreamed that life was Beauty;
I woke, and found that life was Duty. — HOOPER

Great is the art of beginning, but greater the art is of ending. — LONGFELLOW

Opinions shape ideals, and it is ideals that inspire conduct. — JOHN MORLEY

You cannot dream yourself into a character; you must hammer and forge yourself into one. — FROUDE

Not once or twice in our fair island story
The path of duty was the way to glory. — TENNYSON

Know thy work and do it, and work at it like a Hercules. One monster there is in the world — an idle man. — CARLYLE

Every evil to which we do not succumb is a benefactor. We gain the strength of the temptation we resist. — EMERSON

In every common hour of life,
In every flame that glows,
In every breath of being rife
With aspiration or of strife
Man feels more than he knows. — W. W. CAMPBELL

Never to the bow that bends
Comes the arrow that it sends;
Never comes the chance that passed:
That one moment was its last.

Oh, fear not in a world like this,
And thou shalt know ere long,
Know how sublime a thing it is
To suffer and be strong.—H. W. LONGFELLOW

Sow an act, and reap a tendency; sow a tendency, and reap a habit; sow a habit, and reap a character; sow a character, and reap a destiny.—THACKERAY

The gifts that we have, heaven lends for right using, and not for ignoring, and not for abusing.

It is not what he has, nor even what he does, which directly expresses the worth of a man, but what he is.—*Journal*—AMIEL

My good blade carves the casques of men,
My tough lance thrusteth sure,
My strength is as the strength of ten,
Because my heart is pure.—TENNYSON

True worth is in *being*, not *seeming*,—
In doing each day that goes by
Some little good—not in the dreaming
Of great things to do by and by.

No work which God sets a man to do—no work to which God has specially adapted a man's powers—can properly be called either menial or mean.—CARLYLE

Truth, crushed to earth, shall rise again;
Th' eternal years of God are hers;
But Error, wounded, writhes in pain,
And dies among his worshippers.—BRYANT

To thine own self be true;
And it must follow, as the night the day,
Thou can'st not then be false to any man.—SHAKESPEARE

No life
Can be pure in its purpose or strong in its strife
And all life not be purer and stronger thereby.—LYTTON

Knowledge and wisdom far from being one, have ofttimes no connection. Knowledge is proud that he has learned so much; wisdom is humble that he knows no more.—COWPER

Wish not to taste what doth not to thee fall;
Do well thyself, before thou striv'st to lead,
And truth shall thee deliver without dread.—GEOFFREY CHAUCER

Oh, many a shaft, at random sent,
Finds mark the archer little meant!
And many a word at random spoken,
May soothe, or wound, a heart that's broken.—SIR W. SCOTT

Govern the lips as they were palace doors, the king within. Tranquil and fair and courteous be all words which from that presence win.—EDWIN ARNOLD

Whene'er a noble deed is wrought,
Whene'er is spoken a noble thought,
Our hearts, in glad surprise,
To higher levels rise.—LONGFELLOW

Love thyself last; cherish those hearts that hate thee;
Corruption wins not more than honesty.
Still in thy right hand carry gentle peace,
To silence envious tongues; be just, and fear not.—SHAKESPEARE

Not by the power of commerce, art, or pen,
Shall our great Empire stand, nor has it stood,
But by the noble deeds of noble men—
Heroic lives and heroes' outpoured blood.—F. G. SCOTT

Take up the white man's burden—
In patience to abide,
To veil the threat of terror
And check the show of pride;
By open speech and simple,
An hundred times made plain,
To seek another's profit
And work another's gain.—KIPLING

Love thou thy land, with love far-brought
From out the storied Past, and used
Within the Present, but transfused
Thro' future time by power of thought.—TENNYSON

For as long as conquest holds the earth,
Or commerce sweeps the sea,
By orient jungle or western plain
Will the Saxon spirit be;
And whatever the people that dwell beneath,
Or whatever the alien tongue,
Over the freedom and peace of the world
Is the flag of England flung.—W. W. CAMPBELL

Of old sat Freedom on the heights,
The thunders breaking at her feet;
Above her shook the starry lights;
She heard the torrents meet.
Her open eyes desire the truth.
The wisdom of a thousand years
Is in them. May perpetual youth
Keep dry their light from tears.—TENNYSON

If I have faltered more or less
In my great task of happiness;
If I have moved among my race
And shown no glorious morning face;
If beams from happy, human eyes
Have moved me not; if morning skies,
Books, and my food, and summer rain
Knocked on my sullen heart in vain—
Lord, Thy most pointed pleasure take,
And stab my spirit broad awake.—R. L. STEVENSON

A good book is the precious life-blood of a master-spirit, embalmed and treasured up on purpose to a life beyond life.—MILTON

The book which makes a man think the most is the book which strikes the deepest root in his memory and understanding.

Men at some time are masters of their fates:
The fault, dear Brutus, is not in our stars,
But in ourselves, that we are underlings.—SHAKESPEARE

No book is worth anything which is not worth *much;* nor is it serviceable until it has been read and re-read, and loved, and loved again; and marked, so that you can refer to the passages you want in it, as a soldier can seize the weapon he needs in an armoury, or a housewife bring the spice she needs from her store. Bread of flour is good; but there is bread, sweet as honey, if we would eat it, in a good book.—RUSKIN

Goodness moves in a larger sphere than justice. The obligations of law and equity reach only to mankind, but kindness and beneficence should be extended to creatures of every species.—PLUTARCH

My heart leaps up when I behold
A rainbow in the sky;
So was it when my life began,
So is it now I am a man,
So be it when I shall grow old,
Or let me die.
The child is father of the man;
And I could wish my days to be
Bound each to each by natural piety.—WORDSWORTH

Be but yourself, be pure, be true,
And prompt in duty; heed the deep
Low voice of conscience; through the ill
And discord round about you, keep
Your faith in human nature still.—ELIZABETH WHITTIER

Four things a man must learn to do
If he would make his record true;
To think, without confusion, clearly;
To love his fellow-men sincerely:
To act from honest motives purely;
To trust in God and Heaven securely.—HENRY VAN DYKE

Give thy thoughts no tongue,
Nor any unproportioned thought his act.
Be thou familiar, but by no means vulgar;
The friends thou hast, and their adoption tried,
Grapple them to thy soul with hooks of steel.—SHAKESPEARE

Never do anything of which you will have cause to be ashamed. There is one good opinion which is of the greatest importance to you, namely, your own. "An easy conscience", says Seneca, "is a continual feast".—LUBBOCK

There is a tide in the affairs of men,
Which, taken at the flood, leads on to fortune;
Omitted, all the voyage of their life
Is bound in shallows and in miseries.
On such a full sea are we now afloat;
And we must take the current when it serves,
Or lose our ventures.—SHAKESPEARE

Man is his own star, and the soul that can
Render an honest and a perfect man,
Commands all light, all influence, all fate,
Nothing for him falls early or too late;
Our acts our angels are, for good or ill;
Our fatal shadows that walk by us still.—BEAUMONT AND FLETCHER

Our birth is but a sleep and a forgetting;
The soul that rises with us, our life's star,
Hath had elsewhere its setting,
And cometh from afar,
Not in entire forgetfulness,
And not in utter nakedness,
But trailing clouds of glory do we come
From God who is our home.—WORDSWORTH

Be wise to-day; 'tis madness to defer;
Next day the fatal precedent will plead;
Thus on, till-wisdom is pushed out of life.
Procrastination is the thief of time;
Year after year it steals, till all are fled,
And to the mercies of a moment leaves
The vast concerns of an eternal scene.—EDWARD YOUNG

Build thee more stately mansions, O my soul,
As the swift seasons roll!
Leave thy low-vaulted past!
Let each new temple, nobler than the last,

Shut thee from heaven with a dome more vast,
Till thou at length art free,
Leaving thine outgrown shell by life's unresting sea.—O. W. HOLMES

Grow old along with me!
The best is yet to be,
The last of life for which the first was made:
Our times are in His hand
Who saith, "A whole I planned,
Youth shows but half; trust God: see all nor be afraid!" —BROWNING

Were a star quenched on high,
For ages would its light,
Still travelling downward from the sky,
Shine on our mortal sight.
So when a great man dies,
For years beyond our ken,
The light he leaves behind him lies
Upon the paths of men. —LONGFELLOW

It is not growing like a tree
In bulk doth make man better be;
Or standing long, an oak, three hundred year,
To fall a log at last, dry, bald, and sear.
A lily of a day
Is fairer far in May,
Although it fall and die that night—
It was the plant and flower of light.
In small proportions we just beauties see;
And in short measures life may perfect be.—BEN JONSON

We shape ourselves the joy or fear
Of which the coming life is made,
And fill our Future's atmosphere
With sunshine or with shade.
The tissue of the Life to be,
We weave with colours all our own;
And in the field of Destiny
We reap as we have sown.—WHITTIER

Heaven is not reached at a single bound,
But we build the ladder by which we rise
From the lowly earth to the vaulted skies,
And we mount to its summit round by round.
I count this thing to be grandly true:
That a noble deed is a step toward God,—
Lifting the soul from the common clod
To a purer air and a broader view.—J. G. HOLLAND

Let me but do my work from day to day
In field or forest, at the desk or loom,
In roaring market-place or tranquil room;
Let me but find it in my heart to say,
When vagrant wishes beckon me astray,
"This is my work; my blessing, not my doom;
Of all who live, I am the only one by whom
The work can best be done in the right way."—HENRY VAN DYKE

Good name, in man or woman, dear, my lord,
Is the immediate jewel of their soul.
Who steals my purse, steals trash; 'tis something, nothing;
'Twas mine, 'tis his, and has been slave to thousands;
But he that filches from me my good name,
Robs me of that which not enriches him,
And makes me poor indeed.—SHAKESPEARE

God give us men! A time like this demands
Strong minds, great hearts, true faith, and ready hands;
Men whom the lust of office does not kill;
Men whom the spoils of office cannot buy;
Men who possess opinions and a will;
Men who have honour,—men who will not lie.—J. G. HOLLAND

To live content with small means; to seek elegance rather than luxury, and refinement rather than fashion; to be worthy, not respectable; and wealthy, not rich; to study hard, think quietly, talk gently, act frankly; to listen to stars and birds, babes and sages with open heart; await occasions, hurry never; in a word, to let the spiritual, unbidden and unconscious, grow up through the common,—this is my symphony.—CHANNING

O, may I join the choir invisible
Of those immortal dead who live again
In minds made better by their presence; live
In pulses stirred to generosity,
In deeds of daring rectitude, in scorn
Of miserable aims that end with self,
In thoughts sublime that pierce the night like stars,
And with their mild persistence urge men's minds
To vaster issues.—GEORGE ELIOT

A thing of beauty is a joy forever:
Its loveliness increases; it will never
Pass into nothingness; but still will keep
A bower quiet for us, and a sleep
Full of sweet dreams, and health, and quiet breathing.—KEATS

Sunset with its rosy feet
Stains the grasses low and sweet;
And the shadow-beeches softly fall
Across the meadows, dark and tall;
O fold away
The dusty day,
Sweet nightfall, in thy curtains gray.—JAPANESE

Now fades the last long streak of snow,
Now bourgeons every maze of quick
About the flowering squares, and thick
By ashen roots the violets blow.
Now rings the woodland loud and long,
The distance takes a lovelier hue,
And drowned in yonder living blue
The lark becomes a sightless song.—TENNYSON

A cloud lay cradled near the setting sun;
A gleam of crimson tinged its braided snow;
Long had I watched the glory moving on
O'er the still radiance of the lake below.
Tranquil its spirit seemed, and floated slow!
Even in its very motion there was rest;
While every breath of eve that chanced to blow
Wafted the traveller to the beauteous west.—WILSON

Printed by Libri Plureos GmbH in Hamburg,
Germany

9 789361 387722